THE
GOD
WITHIN

Harry R. Klocker, S.J.

UNIVERSITY
PRESS OF
AMERICA

200149

COPYRIGHT ACKNOWLEDGEMENTS

Cornell University Press: for selections from John Hick, Faith and Knowledge, second edition, copyright (c) 1966 by Cornell University, used by permission of the publisher, Cornell University Press.

Harper & Row, Publishers, Inc.: Pierre Teilhard de Chardin, The Future of Man, translated by Norman Denny. Copyright (c) 1964, Harper and Row, Inc., New York.

The Last Years: Journals 1853-1855 by Søren Kierkegaard, edited and translated by Ronald Gregor Smith. Copyright (c) 1965 by Ronald Gregor Smith.

The Phenomenon of Man by Pierre Teilhard de Chardin, translated by Bernard Wall. Copyright (c) 1955 by Editions du Seuil. English translation copyright (c) 1959 by Wm. Collins Sons & Co. Ltd., London and Harper & Row, Publishers, Inc., New York.

The Iliff Review: for use of the article, "A God for Naturalism," H. R. Klocker, S.J., published in the Fall, 1974 issue.

Macmillan Publishing Col, Inc.: for The Meaning of Revelation, H. Richard Neibuhr. Copyright 1941 by Macmillan Publishing Co., Inc. renewed 1969 by Florence Neibuhr, Cynthia M. Niebuhr and Richard R. Niebuhr.

The Modern Schoolman: for "From Rationalism to Faith: Ockham and Kierkegaard," H. R. Klocker, S.J., Volume LV, No. 1 (November 1977) pp. 57-70.

University of Notre Dame Press: for selections from Christ and Prometheus, William J. Lynch. Copyright 1970, University of Notre Dame Press, Notre Dame, Indiana 46556.

Pacific Philosophical Quarterly for permission to reprint "The Personal God of John Henry Newman," H. R. Klocker, S.J., (Personalist, Spring, 1976).

ACKNOWLEDGEMENTS

I also wish to express special thanks to Patricia Hickey for typing the original manuscript, to Grace Jablonski for the final copy, and to Julia Hansen for her work on the index.

I am also grateful to the Rev. Francis C. Wade, S.J. of Marquette University for reading and criticizing the manuscript.

TABLE OF CONTENTS

INTRODUCTION

It is an historical fact that since Immanuel Kant (1724 - 1804) the interest in attempting to establish the existence of God by means of demonstrative proof has radically declined. It is almost taken as a philosophic axiom that Kant once and for all showed the necessary inadequacy of all such attempts. One can, of course, disagree with Kant, and it has been pointed out that the arguments for God's existence which Kant criticized were not in fact those of Aquinas or Scotus or Bonaventure. They were rather a highly rationalistic version of such proofs which were passed on to Kant through the manuals of scholastic philosophy by C. Wolff and A. G. Baumgarten. However that may be, the fact remains that the Kantian position with regard to the impossibility of demonstrative proof has been widely accepted.

The reaction which followed upon the Kantian critique was varied. It included scepticism on the one hand with a new interest in and emphasis on physical and social science and, on the other, a retreat to religious faith and personal conviction as being of more worth than any argument. This latter position had the advantage of putting the believing and religious minded theist on a level where scepticism and scientific attack could not touch him. One of the main difficulties with such a retreat was that it often degenerated into sheer piety or sentimentality where emotion became the essence of religious belief and where reason and intelligence had little or no part to play. It came pretty close at times to reducing theism to wishful thinking or to the simple affirmation that the heart has reasons which the reason knows not of.

Now whatever one may think of demonstrative proof for God's existence, - and I am convinced that there is such proof - the fact remains that there can also be an approach based on the subject which can lead to a reasoned and reasonable affirmation of the existence of God. St. Thomas himself states that most people who call themselves theists do not reach their conviction of God's existence by means of metaphysical argument. There must, then, be other ways. And however much these other ways may fall away from the strict demands of demonstrative proof, many of them are reasoned expressions of a theistic position acceptable to many.

It is the purpose of this book to provide some understanding and an analysis of such positions as exemplified in the writings of various philosophers and theologians who saw the subjective and personal approach to God as not only valuable but convincing. The approaches differ, as one might expect, and the reader will not find all of them equally acceptable or persuasive. There is a vast difference, for example, between the faith of a Kierkegaard and the naturalism of a Bernhardt.

However, there is also a common factor in all of them. It is man's continuing search to find a reasonable answer to the question: Does a Supreme Being exist? That question is by no means limited to professional philosophers and theologians. It is one which confronts any human being who reflects on himself and the world in which humans live and act. In the following pages the reader will meet some of the people who faced that question and answered it affirmatively.

Harry R. Klocker, S.J.
Marquette University
August, 1981

THE PERSONAL GOD OF JOHN HENRY NEWMAN

In his approach to God, Cardinal Newman is always more concerned with why people assent to God's existence than he is with the arguments which have been proposed historically to prove that existence. He himself was greatly influenced at an early age by the Calvinstic doctrine of divine election long before he became acquainted with philosophical proofs for God's existence. He does not deny that such arguments may be valid and even necessary. He knew at least some of them, e.g., those proposed by Butler and Paley.[1] If he is skeptical about the arguments for God's existence based on design in the universe, it is for very good reasons. In the first place, Newman is very much dissatisfied with the notion of causality as it is employed in the design argument.

ORIGIN OF THE NOTION OF CAUSALITY

Newman never doubts that the causal proposition is valid. Neither is he a rationalist, when he describes how it happens that one becomes aware of the connection between effect and cause. In the _Grammar of Assent_,[2] he indicates clearly that our knowledge of causality is grounded in a twofold personal experience. In the first place, the notion of cause is derived from the experience we have of willing to perform certain actions and the ability we have to transfer this will into practice. There seems to be here an actual exercise of causality flowing from the will of the self into the external activity performed by that same self. I will to raise my arm, and I do raise it. I choose to walk across the room, and I am capable of translating that choice into the external activity of walking. It is from such personal experience that one comes to know what cause and effect mean.

This is, furthermore, no sophisticated awareness developed only after years of trying to explain the constant association between the events of one's experience. On the contrary, it is one of the first experiences

that we all have as children. 'Infants' is the word
he uses.[3] It is this awareness of arbitrary power over
one's actions that leads a boy to test and express it,
even at the price of disobedience and punishment.

Another sort of experience arises from such
exercise of one's causal power. This second experience
further expands and deepens the personal awareness we
all possess of cause and effect. For the child, in
exercising the power that is his, is brought up short
at times by the opposition of his parents to his activity. He is restrained, reprimanded, forbidden to act
in a certain way. His will is opposed by the will of
others and that for reasons contrary to his own. Hence,
Newman can argue that from the earliest years the awareness of causality is always connected with purpose and
will and, therefore, with intelligent agents.

This is the basic causal experience for Newman,
and beyond this, we can claim no awareness of causality.[4] That is why, among primitive peoples, the
physical forces at work in nature are always ascribed
to the will and desire of hidden agents and not the
things themselves.[5] We have no knowledge of whether
or how mere things exercise activity on one another,
but we are aware of our own personal activity which
flows from our will to act.

Starting, then, from experience, I consider a cause
to be an effective will; and, by the doctrine of
causation, I mean the notion, or first principle,
that all things come from effective will; and the
reception or presumption of this notion is a notional assent.[6]

Newman is far removed here from any abstract
analysis of the terms 'cause' and 'effect'. Nor would
he think of deriving the causal principle from the
principle of non-contradiction, or from the notion of
finite being. There is no similarity at all between
the notion of causality, as Newman understands it, and
the so-called principle of sufficient reason. The
principle of sufficient reason might lead to the estab-
lishment of scientific law, but it could never substitute for a real cause. Even when he speaks of receiv-

ing the notion of causality with notional, as opposed to real, assent, Newman is speaking of the universalization of causality and not of its concrete discovery in our own personal experience. On the contrary, the assent we give to the reality of the causality we exercise in our personal internal and external activity is a real assent grounded in the awareness of what we are doing.

Admittedly, Newman is not attempting a justification or a proof of the universal validity of the causal proposition. He is not sure that such a proof could be given. He is simply asserting that the awareness of cause and effect is present from the very early stages of consciousness. This consciousness is radically an awareness of our own causal activity, but it is also modified and limited by the awareness we have of others. But in either case, the awareness of cause and effect is connected with purpose and will and, accordingly, with intelligent agents or persons. Hence, there is no need for Newman to demonstrate, in the Aristotelian sense, the validity of the causal proposition.

THE BACKGROUND OF NEWMAN'S POSITION

THE ANSWER TO HUME

It is no secret that Newman had great admiration for Locke, and it is equally clear that he was aware of Hume and the philosophical skepticism which logically resulted from Hume's position. This is especially apparent in Hume's theory of causality. It is hardly necessary here to review again in detail Hume's philosophy of cause and effect.[7] Suffice it to say that Hume denied any possible experience of a causal influx and thus reduced the meaning of causality to a mere constant association of ideas. Hence, for Hume causality means only a de facto concomitance of certain ideas, which ideas we ordinarily find associated in experience.[8] Since past experience is in no way a certain ground for future experience, the most that Hume could grant was a predictability for the future with relation to the past.

3

Newman's reply to the Humean position was partly an acceptance of it and partly a denial--especially of what he considered its inadequacy. He clearly accepted Hume's teaching that in our experience of things we do not and cannot directly apprehend a causal influx. "Physical phenomena are as such without sense; and experience teaches us nothing about physical phenomena as causes."[9] But Newman just as clearly rejected this as the only possibility of experiencing cause and effect. As we have already seen, he insists that there is a direct experience of causality, as given in the immediate grasp of our own causal efficacy. What Newman is saying is that Hume is correct in denying that our experience of things can provide us with the validity of the causal proposition. On the other hand, Hume has not pushed his experimental investigation far enough. There is another area of experience which needs to be looked at--the area of will and its immediate effect in experience. It is here that we know we are causes, and it is here that we do experience what we mean by causality. It is only fair to admit that Hume had an answer to this;[10] but so did Newman. People in general accept the validity of the causal proposition. There is no question in most people's minds that they are causes responsible for their own actions. It is a common experience, for example, that all of us think we deserve praise when we have performed an act of kindness or made a success of a job entrusted to us. In the same way, we hold ourselves responsible for activities that did not succeed, or for actions that produced inadequate or even bad results. Why? There must be some reason for this attitude. And Newman's answer to Hume is direct and clear. We know that we habitually exercise causal activity.

DISTINCTION BETWEEN CAUSALITY AND SCIENTIFIC LAW

Newman's identification of causality with will and purpose led him naturally to question the causality of the non-personal elements in the material universe. When we speak of causality on this level, we are doing so only by analogy with the notion of cause and effect we have experienced in our own activities. Since causality always implies sequence, and since we experience antecedents and consequents in nature, we call the former the cause of the latter. We do this even though intelligence and will are absent in the things of nature.[11] Newman concedes Hume's position in this area, at least insofar as direct experience of causality as such in the material universe is concerned.

This analogical application of cause and effect to material things results finally in confusing causality with order. For order, according to Newman, is nothing else but the attempt to interrelate happenings in nature, formulate hypotheses to explain their interrelation, and thus to establish laws for natural science. But it should be recognized that such laws are abstractions and merely the formulae under which the phenomena of nature are conveniently represented. There is no direct experience of such laws. On the contrary, what is experienced is always unique, always slightly different, and never an exact expression of the law according to which the phenomena are supposed to operate. The most that can be said here is that there is enough uniformity in nature to enable us to grasp a relationship between antecedents and consequents. This relationship, however, remains an abstract and general approximation to what actually happens. This is called law, or order, but it would certainly be a confusion to identify such formulae with causes.

CAUSALITY AND THE EXISTENCE OF GOD

It is easy to see that Newman can have little to do with many of the so-called arguments for the existence of God based on physical causality. As has been pointed out, Newman was skeptical about the possibility of establishing the reality of cause and effect in the physical universe. But over and beyond this, the argument from physical causality, or the argument from design, had also come under serious attack by men such as Mill and Darwin. Newman himself found the argument completely unconvincing. He thought it much too narrow an approach for one thing, and that it left the whole concept of God much too ambiguous for another. In a letter to Brownlow, he stated that he believed in design because he believed in God; not in God because he saw design.[12]

Newman was also aware of both Hume's and Kant's objections to the argument. Hume had argued that such

5

an argument based on physical causality--dubious as
that supposition is--could prove no more than a being
or beings possessing that precise degree of power, intelligence, and benevolence, which appears in the work
it, or they, are supposed to have produced. Any further
attributes predicated of such a being would be mere
hypothesis.[13] Kant, too, had harshly criticized the
argument, contending that at best it proved a Great
Designer and not a God. Furthermore, he had argued
that any attempt to make the transition from such a
Designer to an absolute or necessary Being always fell
back into the ontological argument, which was also in-
valid.[14]

Newman is also afraid that the argument has further difficulties. What is meant by the 'God' that it
supposes to prove? It is quite possible that the word
'God' here is simply a substitute for 'chance' or 'fate'.
Or it may be that 'God' is only a term standing for the
abstract laws which are conceived as immanent to nature
itself. He is unwilling to settle for a God who may be
just a generalization of phenomena.[15]

Newman would much rather speak of order than
design; for order implies purpose, and purpose, in turn,
intellect and will. In this way he is back to cause,
as he had previously defined it: an effective will that
operates through intelligence. Once someone is convinced of the existence of God, he can also be convinced
that God orders the world and everything in it to an
intelligent end. In place of the impersonal, abstract,
physical cause of those who argue from design, Newman
is able to substitute a personal Supreme Being who wills
the world intelligently and who has a direct and immediate control over it. Furthermore, such a God is able
to demand from us a real and not just a notional assent
on all levels: philosophical, moral, and religious.

In finding his own way toward God, Newman turned
to the human individual. What is it in the individual,
or at least in most individuals, which leads them to
assent to the existence of a Supreme Being? This assent is always unqualified, although the proposition to
which assent is given need not be. To understand such
absolute and certain assent to the proposition, God

exists, we must first look at what Newman means by
'assent' and how it fits into the psychological process.

NATURE OF ASSENT

The object of the mind's assent is always a proposition. Such propositions are formulated by the mind
and may refer to facts of experience, in which case
they are called real propositions. The propositions
may also express a conclusion from other propositions;
in this case they are called notional propositions.
The assent which the mind gives to each type of proposition will itself be named a real or a notional assent.
It is important to note here that a real assent always
involves more than a notional assent. In a real assent
there is always more than just the intellect. In such
an act of assent there is a relation to experience and
to images; the senses enter in to the extent they can;
emotion is involved; so that the act of assent tends to
commit the whole person and not just the mind. Newman
expresses the difference as follows:

> An act of assent, it seems, is the most perfect and
> highest of its kind, when it is exercised on propo-
> sitions, which are apprehended as experiences and
> images, that is, which stand for things; and on the
> other hand, an act of inference is the most perfect
> and highest of its kind, when it is exercised on
> propositions which are apprehended as notions, that
> is, which are creations of the mind.[16]

Newman does, however, sound a warning. The brilliance
of the images involved or the intensity of emotion connected with a real assent to a proposition is no guarantee of the proposition's truth. Reason must remain
the directive factor. But it is also true that reason
taken by itself, abstracted from the life situation,
has very little power of persuasion. Newman had little
sympathy for logic, and he thought life was too short
for a religion of inference. "We shall never have
done beginning, if we determine to begin with proof."[17]

THE PROBLEM

Newman's problem, then, is to find a factual
source, clearly experiential, which will lead to a real
assent to the proposition: There is a God. The evidence

must be such that it will involve the imagination and
the emotion and commit the individual to the reality of
God so that this Divine Reality becomes a directive
force in life's activity. Furthermore, the argument, if
it is one,[18] must have certain definite characteristics
since it will constitute at least the implicit source
of why most men are theists rather than atheists. Hence,
the reasoning will have to be fitting for every man. It
must be fundamental and personal, for it has to involve
the whole man. It must also lead to a God who is not
so vague nor abstract as to make the theist's assent
almost meaningless.[19]

Can one, then attain to a more vivid assent to
the Being of a God, than that which is given merely to
notions of the intellect? Can I enter with personal
knowledge into the circle of truths which make up that
great thought? Can I believe as if I saw? Since such
an assent requires a present experience or memory of
the fact, and since no one in this life can see God,
how is such an assent possible? Nevertheless, Newman
thinks it is.[20] He proceeds as follows.

PRESUMPTIONS TO THE ARGUMENT
By 'presumption' Newman means an assent to first
principles. And by a first principle he means the propositions with which we start in reasoning on any given
subject matter.[21] The term is a very broad one. Such
basic propositions are quite numerous and vary in great
measure with the persons who reason. They are notional
propositions, not images; they express what is abstract;
and they are very often implicit. Among the most common are the propositions that we exist, that we have
certain faculties, that there is an external world,
that the intellect can achieve truth.

Newman's radical point of departure is the consciousness of his own existence. Although he calls
this a presumption, he is careful to note that it is
not a gratuitous starting point. The awareness that I
am is not susceptible of formal inference, nor can it be.
Neither is it the object of an act of faith, since no
one believes what is immediately evident. Nor is the
object of such awareness a simple being. I am aware of
my existence through my acts of thinking, remembering,

8

sensing. Hence, one could just as easily use "Sentio, ergo sum" or "Cogito, ergo sum". In other words, to affirm that I am aware of my own existence is to affirm that I am a thinking, reasoning, sensing being. I know myself and my own existence through my acts, and these acts are varied and complex. All these facets of the kind of being I am are implicitly included in the primary awareness and can be explicated in simple propositions later. To question this basic presumption is for Newman to give up the game before it starts. I am what I am and there is no other criterion by which I can measure that assertion outside of my own awareness of myself.

CONSCIENCE AS A UNIQUE ACT OF SELF_AWARENESS
        In general, reason is the source of consciousness and self-awareness, so that to say that I am what I am is to assert that I am a reasonable being. Now reason includes many acts, but unique among these acts is that of conscience. In the manuscript, The Proof of Theism, Newman defines conscience as the discrimination of acts as worthy of praise or blame. Such discrimination has a double facet. Not only am I aware of breaking or abserving a law, but that the law says this or that. The second aspect of conscience may change. In other words, my conscience may be mistaken about a particular instance, or about how the law should be followed in a given case. But the first aspect of conscience always remains. I am under a law by which I am judged, by which I shall be called to account. It is in this sense that conscience is a sanction which no one can ever escape and which is as much a part of his being as is reason itself. Hence, it is just as true to say that I am conscious that I am the kind of being who walks accountable as it is to say I am conscious that I am.[22]

CONSCIENCE DISTINGUISHED FROM GOOD TASTE
        The sense of the beautiful has no special relation to persons but considers acts in themselves. Taste is its own evidence, appealing to nothing beyond its own sense of the beautiful or ugly, and enjoying specimens of the beautiful simply for their own sake. Conscience, however, always reaches beyond itself and at least directly discerns a sanction higher than itself

for its decisions. The evidence for this is that keen
sense of obligation and responsibility which informs
such decisions. That is why we can speak of conscience
as a voice, a term we never think of applying to the
sense of the beautiful. This voice, moreover, is imperative and constraining like no other dictate in the
whole of our experience.[23]

Newman realizes, however, that if the dictate of
conscience is to be identified with a personal God,
then there has to be still more involved in our relation
to it than has up to this time been indicated. Conscience must lead us beyond ourselves, not just to an
impersonal or abstract command, but to a living Person.
In the Grammar of Assent,[24] Newman indicates that this
is precisely the case. For the act of conscience is
the only one of our mental acts which is closely associated with our emotions. Conscience leads us to rever-
ence and awe, to hope, and especially to fear. Now fear
is foreign to good taste and even to particular violations of the moral sense. But if one has been betrayed
into any kind of immorality, he has a lively sense of
responsibility and guilt. This is true, even if the
act be no offense against society. There is distress
and apprehension, even though the act was beneficial to
its perpetrator. There is compunction and regret, even
though the act was most pleasurable. There is confusion of face, even though there were no witnesses.[25]

Conscience, then, is always emotional. It always involves the recognition of a living object toward
which it is directed. Inanimate things cannot stir our
affections; these are correlative with persons. If we
are ashamed, are frightened, feel responsible at trans-
gressing the voice of conscience, this implies that
there is One to whom we are responsible, before whom we
are ashamed, whose claims on us we fear.[26]

Newman sees a parallel in man's reaching out to
a transcendent God behind the dictate of conscience and
other such recognitions we are all familiar with in the
natural order. Animals, for example, discern unities
under the shifting shapes and colors of the visible
world. They cannot do this by reason, since they have
no reason. It can hardly be attributed to sense, since

the senses are directed to phenomena, not to the perception of unified entities. Yet, the animals do seek
out individuals and even seem to recognize the personality of their master. Newman attributes this quite
natural happening, mysterious as it is, to an instinct.
How are we to explain such an instinct, whether it be
in the case of brutes or again of children?

> But until we account for the knowledge which an in-
> fant has of its mother or its nurse, what reason have
> we to take exception at the doctrine, so strange and
> difficult, that in the dictate of conscience, with-
> out previous experience or analogical reasoning, he
> is able gradually to perceive the voice, or the
> echoes of the voice, of a Master, living, personal,
> and sovereign?[27]

ORIGIN OF CONSCIENCE

That conscience is connatural to our human nature
is particularly exemplified in the case of a child. For
a child at the age of four or five has some clear, basic
religious principles on which he acts. When he does
wrong, he is conscious that he is offending One to whom
he is answerable, whom he does not see, who sees him.
His mind reaches out to the thought of a Moral Governor,
sovereign over him, mindful and just. It comes to him
like an impulse of nature to entertain it. Newman admits that it would be difficult to determine how far
such initial knowledge comes from outside and how far
from within, how much is natural and how much is due to
divine aid. But this is hardly to the point. He is
not trying to trace the image of God to its first
origins in man, but simply trying to show that a child
can become possessed of such an image. This image,
then, becomes the foundation on which a real assent to
God as a person is based. Depending on circumstances,
it can grow, become more mature, more attractive, and
can lead the individual to an even greater dedication
to a personal God and an even more profound commitment
to following the dictates of his conscience.

It is not just in the child that Newman finds conscience as a natural concomitant to his developing mind.
Conscience is there in the history of the developing
human species itself teaching primitive man of all

classes and all conditions that there is a God and what He is like. But the most basic information which conscience gives about God is that He is our Judge. We learn from conscience to conceive of God, not primarily as a God of Wisdom, of Knowledge, of Power, of Benevolence, but as a God of Judgment and Justice. This God ordains that the offender should suffer for his offense, not just for his own good, but as a good in itself. The God, then, who is presented to us by nature is a God who is angry with us and who threatens evil.

If it tells us anything at all of the characteristics of the Divine Mind, it certainly tells us this; and considering that our shortcomings are far more frequent and important than our fulfillment of the duties enjoining upon us, and that of this point we are fully aware ourselves, it follows that the aspect under which Almighty God is presented to us by nature, is (to use a figure) of One who is angry with us, and threatens evil.[28]

The history of primitive religion is only a confirmation of this. Wherever religion exists in a popular shape, it has almost invariably worn its dark side outward. It is always grounded in a sense of sin; and without that vivid sense it would hardly have any precepts or observances. The proclamation is there that man is in a degraded, servile condition, and requires expiation, reconciliation, and some great change of nature.

This is suggested to us in the many ways in which we are told of a realm of light and a realm of darkness, of an elect fold and regenerate state. It is suggested in the almost ubiquitous and ever-recurring institution of a Priesthood; for wherever there is a priest, there is the notion of sin, pollution, and retribution, as, on the other hand, of intercession and mediation. Also, still more directly, is the notion of our guilt impressed upon us by the doctrine of future punishment, and that eternal, which is found in mythologies and creeds of such various parentage.[29]

Conscience, then, has been at work in history, indicating to man that he is guilty, alienated, ordered to judgment before an existing God. The evidence that man is aware of his condition is amply expressed by his attempts at placation, his rites of propitiation, his hopes for betterment, his pleas for mercy and forgiveness. Newman insists again in his Proof of Theism that this is no mere abstract law, no impersonal command. Just as thinking involves existence, so this particular function of thought called conscience points to a personal obligation imposed on me by a Personal Being who calls me to account. Again, he contrasts this experience with good taste and finds no sanction connected with the notions of the beautiful or the ugly. There is no hope or fear associated with taste, no misgiving of the future, no tender sorrow. It is precisely these feelings which carry the mind out of itself and beyond itself, which imply a tribunal in the future, and reward and punishment which are so special.[30]

THE ARGUMENT AND CERTITUDE

Such is Newman's argument for the existence of God based on the testimony of the human conscience. He admits readily that it is not a metaphysical argument nor one that can be validated according to the rules of scientific reasoning, yet he also maintains that the argument can be a certain one and that it can lead to an unconditional and indefectible assent. How this is possible is the point at issue throughout the Grammar of Assent. He states flatly that it is a pretentious axiom that probable reasoning can never lead to certitude.[31] As a matter of fact, most of our most certain judgments are based on propositions which, if examined according to the rules of formal inference, could be regarded as only probably true.

According to Newman, assent is always unconditional. It is called simple assent when given to a proposition relating to concrete fact. Such an assent can be spontaneous, elicited by immediate evidence, involved with sense experience. It need not be reflective. The certitude connected with such an assent is only implicit. Assent, however, may also be more complex. It can be given to propositions which are inferred from others. Such propositions are abstract, they

13

require reflection, and the assent elicited is called notional. The certitude accompanying such an assent is always reflective and therefore explicit. The difficulty with such an assent is that it never reaches concrete fact. The problem is how to make an assent to a proposition, such as: There is a God, explicitly certain when the proposition itself is not derived from metaphysical argument, from scientific demonstration, or necessitated absolutely by the rules of logic.

Newman's first step is to indicate the limitations of formal reasoning or inference. This is also called syllogistic reasoning and it is based on the rules of logic. Now the logical method has both advantages and disadvantages. Logic is successful insofar as words can be found for representing the countless varieties of thought. But logic will fail when it relies too heavily on its original assumption that whatever can be thought can be expressed in words. In other words, logic is forced to narrow the meaning of the words, or terms, it makes use of so that one and only one meaning will maintain throughout the course of the argument. This can be done very well in science, in mathematics, and in the abstract. These are the areas where formal inference is strictly at its best. In such instances, inference deals with a narrowed-down, abstract version of the real. Hence, its conclusions are always abstract, never concrete.

The second difficulty with the logical method is that it must make assumptions and can never prove these assumptions. There is an infinite regress possible once we challenge the basic premise on which an argument is based. To prove such a premise requires another basic premise and so on ad infinitum. There is an equally formidable difficulty at the other end. Since the conclusions of an inferential argument is always universal and abstract, it can never deal with concrete facts. Therefore, however valid the argument may be in the abstract, it can only be probable when applied to the concrete and the individual. We just never know that what is said about 'man' in the abstract and universal will be true about George or my father-in-law. Logic fails at both ends--at the point from which the proof should start and the point at which it should arrive. It falls short of both first principles and concrete issues. Both are beyond its reach.[32]

The objection, then, that the argument for the proposition, God exists, is neither metaphysical nor demonstrative, is of little concern to Newman. While he never denies that there could be such an argument for the existence of God, he was well aware that he was not trying to formulate one. As mentioned above, Newman was always more interested in what led people to accept a God than in whether one could construct a formally valid reasoning process.

If logic is not the method by which we become certain of what is concrete, Newman is equally clear about how such certitude is achieved.

It is plain that formal logical sequence is not in fact the method by which we are enabled to become certain of what is concrete; and it is equally plain, from what has been already suggested, what the real and necessary method is. It is the culmination of probabilities, independent of each other, arising out of the nature and circumstances of the particular case which is under review; probabilities too fine to avail separately, too subtle and circuitous to be convertible into syllogisms, too numerous and various for such conversion, even were they convertible. As a man's portrait differs from a sketch of him, in having, not merely a continuous outline, but all its details filled in, and shades and colours laid on and harmonized together, such is the multiform and intricate process of ratiocination, necessary for our reaching him as a concrete fact, compared with the rude operation of syllogistic treatment.[33]

This method of reasoning from the convergence of probabilities has definite characteristics. In the first place, it does not dispense with nor is it opposed to logic or formal inference. In fact, it includes logical inference but it moves on the level of concrete reality and not on that of abstraction. The process is one whose reasoning is implicit rather than explicit, without the full advertence of the mind exercising it. Lastly, the method does not remedy or remove the condi-

15

tional character of inference. Just as in inferential
reasoning, this method is still dependent on premises.
The problem is in a way made more complex. Formal inference, after all, is demonstrative, once the premises
are granted. But an accumulation of probabilities will
vary in number and the estimated value of each separate
proposition. Hence, the truth or probability of a proposition will also vary with the individual intellect
which considers it. Newman proceeds to list several
examples of arguments which lead to certain conclusions,
according to the rules of formal inference.[34]

Yet it is also true that most of the reasoning
we make use of in our daily affairs is of this type.
We consider various reasons, some more probable than
others, some more meaningful and impressive to us personally by reason of our training, background, etc.
Out of such considerations we gradually come to a conclusion through an instinctive perception that, all
things considered, this is the right conclusion to hold.
We do something similar on the level of sense perception.
We grasp an object in our experience as a unified whole,
not in its separate details. We take it in, recognize
it, and discriminate it from other objects all at once.

Thus in concrete reasonings we are in great measure
thrown back into that condition, from which logic
proposed to rescue us. We judge for ourselves, by
our own lights, and on our own principles; and our
criterion of truth is not so much the manipulation
of propositions, as the intellectual and moral character of the person maintaining them, and the ultimate silent effect of his arguments or conclusions
upon our minds.[35]

What Newman has in mind becomes clear once we
apply the method to his argument for the existence of
God based on conscience. We do not move from notion to
notion, from one abstract proposition to another. The
argument does not proceed from an analysis of obligation to the notion of law to that of a lawgiver. It is
rather based on the individual's willingness to open
himself to the ever present living voice of his own
conscience. To this he brings also along with his intelligence his personal experience, his imagination,

his emotions, his hopes and his need to be sustained, directed, etc. The possibility of a living God as the source of the obligation, present to his conscience, must be admitted, even cherished by the man of good will. It is not a question either of reflecting on this God and reducing Him to such abstract intelligibilities of eternity, omniscience, and omnipresence. Rather, it consists in contemplating Him as eternal, all-knowing and always present. The process cannot be forced. But Newman is convinced that, if given the opportunity, the conviction resulting from it will be humanly rewarding in the complete sense, and will lead to a fully human conviction to which a complete and certain assent can be given.[36]

Newman also turns to Locke to confirm his position that there are cases in which evidence, not sufficient for a scientific proof, is nevertheless sufficient for assent and certitude.

He tells us that belief, grounded on sufficient probabilities, "rises to assurance;" and as to the question of sufficiency, that where propositions "border on certainty," then, "we assent to them as firmly as if they were infallibly demonstrated."[37]

Newman, however, goes beyond Locke. Where Locke thought such propositions were few in number, Newman thinks they are to be found throughout the whole range of concrete matter. Furthermore, that supra-logical judgment, which is the warranty for our certitude about them, is not mere common sense, but the true healthy action of our ratiocinative powers, an action more comprehensive than the mere appreciation of a syllogistic argument. These are the judgments made by prudent men in all areas. But like prudence, the ability to do this is not given to human nature generally, but is a personal endowment.[38]

The next question is whether an account can be given of the validity of this method. Now it is sometimes, at least, possible to reduce such a series of propositions to formally valid syllogisms and thus to show that they do constitute demonstrative proofs. But again, Newman is not interested in such reductive validation. He chooses to propose another type of consideration.

This principle of concrete reasoning is parallel to the
method of proof which is the foundation of modern mathematical science. In his Principia, Newton writes that a
regular polygon, inscribed in a circle, its sides being
continually diminished, tends to become that circle, as
its limit. But it vanishes before it has coincided
with the circle, so that its tendency to be the circle,
though nearer fulfillment, never in fact gets beyond a
tendency. In like manner, the conclusion in a real or
concrete question is foreseen and predicted rather than
actually attained.[39] It is by the variety and multiplicity of the premises, by objections overcome, by adverse
theories neutralized, by unlooked-for correlations found
with already established truths, that the experienced
mind is able to be sure that a conclusion is inevitable,
even though he may not be able to make a demonstrative
argument. This is what we mean when we say something
is as good as proved, or that we have reasons amounting
to a proof. For a proof is the limit of converging
probabilities.[40] This is the kind of reasoning that is
used in physics, in literary criticism and in law courts,
as Newman shows by various examples. The proof, for instance, that a person is guilty of a certain crime is
achieved, in the absence of eye-witnesses, by putting
together all sorts of indirect evidence until, finally,
the conclusion is reached that "beyond a reasonable
doubt", the accused is guilty.

THE ILLATIVE SENSE
        It is in the function of what Newman terms the
illative sense that certainty emerges out of the collective probabilities. He rejects Hume's position that
from probable premises certainty is always impossible.
We should accept as a law of our nature what actually
happens on a large scale. Our hoping is proof that
hope is not an extravagance, and our possession of certitude is proof that it is not a weakness or an absurdity to be certain.[41]

        Certitude, then, is a factual state of mind re-
garding one or more propositions. It is not a passive
impression made on the mind from outside, but an active
recognition of propositions as true. It is further a
duty for each individual to make certain assents, when
reason indicates that these are proper. But is there

18

any criterion for the accuracy of such an inference, a warrant for the assent which follows upon it? There is. The sole and final judgment on the validity of an inference in concrete matter is committed to the personal action of the ratiocinative faculty, the perfection of which is called the illative sense.[42]

To the further question--What right do we have to trust such a human function?--Newman's answer is simple and straightforward: Because we are what we are. We live in a world of facts, and we use them. There is nothing else to use. We ourselves are a counterpart to these facts. We reflect and act on them. This consciousness, this awareness and action we call our rationality. This is also a fact. If one can question this or doubt that he exists in a certain way in a certain situation, then he had better let all thinking and inquiry alone. I am what I am or I am nothing. If I do not use myself as I am, I have no other self to use.

This is true not only of man but also of other areas of our experience. Every being is in a very true sense sufficient for itself and what it requires to bring itself to its own limited type of perfection. Plants and animals all have the necessary equipment to become what they are supposed to be, and, barring interference from other sources, will achieve it. If we turn our attention to man, we find that he is a being of progress with relation to his perfection and characteristic good. Other beings possess from the beginning all that they will ever have. But man possesses his initial good only in rudimentary form. Man must be the creator of his own sufficiency. He is to be the architect of his own fulfillment. In fact, he must be, at the price of never becoming fully human.

Now in the case of man this progress is carried out by means of the acquisition of knowledge, of which inference and assent are the immediate instruments. If this is the way we achieve our human stature, then it follows that we have a sacred duty to use these two instruments rightly and properly. If, however, the first of these instruments, i.e., inference, is always obscure and only probable with relation to concrete fact, while assent is always distinct and definite, then what are we

to do but resign ourselves to what we find?[43] Instead
of devising, what cannot be, some sufficient science of
reasoning which may compel certitude in concrete conclusions, what can we do but confess that there is no
ultimate test of truth besides the testimony born to
truth by the mind itself?

The argument itself is highly characteristic of
Newman's concrete approach. We do make certain assents.
These may be vouched for by demonstrative arguments in
the areas which depend on notional inference. But in
the realm of concrete fact, which notional inference
can never really approach, we must be left with assents
to certain real propositions whose ultimate validation
can only be: It must be so because I do not see how it
could be otherwise.

Such a process need not seem strange to us, since
we make use of it in many different areas. How else
does the mind fulfill its function of direction and control in matters of duty, social intercourse, and taste?
An ethical system, for example, may supply laws, general rules, guiding principles, etc., but the individual intellect must still apply them to its own case in
its own unique situation. Where can any of us go in
such a case except to our own living intelligence or to
that of another? No science of life applicable to the
case of each individual ever has been or can be written.
The oracle, if there is one, is seated in the mind of
the individual person who must be his own law, his own
teacher, and his own judge in those special cases of
duty which are personal to him.

Newman is careful to clarify what he is saying
here. The law of truth differs from the law of duty.
Duties may change, even though truth does not. But
though truth is ever one and the same, and the assent
of certitude is immutable, still the reasonings which
carry us on to truth and certitude are many and distinct,
and vary with the inquirer. Everyone acts in this manner in most of the judgments he makes in his practical
life--in matters of taste, in buying and selling, in his
treatment of others, in political decisions, in dangers,
in his recreations and pleasures. Thus it is and not
by science, that he perfects the virtue of justice,

self-command, magnanimity, generosity, and all others.[44]
The implication is clear. Why do we demand demonstrative proof, according to the laws of logic, where an
issue as important as the existence of God is concerned,
when we do not demand it in most other areas of our
lives? There are many areas and many different ways in
which we achieve certitude and are completely satisfied
that it is so. Why should the reasonable and reasoning
human mind make a particular case of the proposition:
God exists?[45]

CONCLUSION
        That, in brief, is Newman's position. The affir-
mation of God's existence is a concrete judgment which
the individual must make in the face of the evidence
which is there to be considered. No one else can make
it for him. At the same time, each man is not unfamil-
iar with such judgments. He makes them constantly in a
wide variety of situations. Furthermore, the evidence
at hand where the existence of God is concerned is not
negligible. First and foremost is the dictate of his
own conscience, which, whether he likes it or not, tells
him that he is personally accountable to Another both
now and in the future. This awareness of accountability
is part and parcel of that wider consciousness and reasoning power which makes man uniquely what he is among
the animals. Hence, in his very being he is ordered to
and dependent upon a Being whose attributes identify
Him as Divine. For again, it is conscience which indicates that this Other must be personal, all-knowing,
with the right to command, and the ability to judge to
what extent each man should be rewarded for his com-
pliance or punished for his negligence.

        Add to this the interpretation and organizing
element which is always involved with conscience and
the individual is prepared for an assent which involves
not just his intellect but his whole person. If that
assent is given and that commitment made, then it is
Newman's contention that conscience will function ever
more profoundly and lead the individual ever more se-
curely toward that God Who alone can make him truly human and responsible, both as an individual and as a
member of society.

21

As was mentioned above, Newman never meant the argument to be metaphysically demonstrative. I agree with J. H. Walgrave that it could be made so. But Newman was much more interested in formulating an argument that would appeal to most men and one whose starting point was readily available. In this I think he was remarkably successful. The reasoning process always moves on the level of the concrete. Most men, too, are aware of the dictates of conscience and the peculiar role that conscience exercises in their moral lives. The argument is also quite existential. It takes man as we find him in the present and points him beyond himself to a present, living source of the accounting he feels bound to give of himself now and in the future. It is true that both good will and an open mind are prerequisites for the argument, but very few men are without these.

The argument is also strikingly contemporary. In a world in which individual and personal freedom is becoming more and more highly prized the argument provides an intelligent option for a theistically centered life. With the values of a materialistic and technological society constantly being challenged, Newman's approach provides for the individual a profoundly personal source from which he can transcend the shallowness he finds all around him. A conscience accountable to God is a better bet for integrity and responsibility, both in the individual and in society, than a whole series of abstract conclusions based either on personal emotion or on secularistic ideals. It poses a thoughtful challenge also to the current superficial attitude that "anything is moral if it doesn't hurt someone else". And it is a decided check on the extreme brand of individualism which makes each individual a law unto himself.

There are difficulties enough to seize upon, if one is of a mind to reject the argument. Newman was aware of most of them. But he seemed to sense that one in particular made an alternate option possible, and he tried to handle that possibility. It is the possibility that one could identify conscience with good taste. If this can be done, then one could opt for secularistic humanism and maintain that he feels himself under the

22

same obligation as one who thinks he is accountable to
a God. In a cultivated and sophisticated age, violations of the dictates of conscience may be passed off
not as sins against a law of God but as simply a lack
of self-discipline. The fear, which implies the transgression of a law laid down by a Lawgiver and a Judge
may turn into mere self-reproach, and self-reproach is
directed and limited to our sense of what is fitting
and becoming.

> . . .conscience tends to become what is called a
> moral sense; the command of duty is a sort of taste;
> sin is not an offense against God, but against hu-
> man nature.[46]

Thus conscience becomes mere self-respect. When one
sins he calls himself a fool. One is embarrassed for
his lack of propriety or good taste. An apology may
well be required, but to oneself, or, perhaps, to one's
hostess, not to God. Newman refers to this as the religion of a philosopher or a gentlemen. It is based upon
honor. Vice is evil because it is unworthy. Conscience
in morals becomes parallel to genius in art and wisdom
in philosophy.[47]

In the Grammar of Assent, Newman distinguished
between conscience and good taste by indicating the completely different emotional impact of conscience and its
transcendent quality. Here in the Idea of a University
his judgment of the inadequacy of good taste is harsher.
Such an attempt to substitute good taste for conscience
is essentially superficial. Its only measure of right
and wrong is visible beauty and tangible fitness. If
we make light of the deeply interior dictate of conscience, there is nothing left but to pay homage to
what is more upon the surface. To seem to be; what
looks fair will be good; what causes offense will be evil.

Whatever else Newman has accomplished, and it has
been much, he has made the God-option a deeply intelligent alternative for one who stands at the crossroads.
He has also given to theism a profoundly personal approach which helps considerably to clarify why most men
are believers. Starting with what is radically personal
to the individual psyche, he attempts to lead the indi-

vidual to a realization that it is only by allowing
himself to be directed beyond himself that he can become truly what he is.

NOTES

[1] William Paley, Natural Theology (Boston: Gold and Lincoln, 1854): John Butler Natural and Revealed Theology (Dover, N.H.: W. Burr, 1861).

[2] John Henry Newman, The Grammar of Assent (Garden City, N.Y.: Image Books, Doubleday and Company, Inc. 1955), p. 70.

[3] Ibid., p. 70.

[4] Ibid.

[5] Ibid., p. 71.

[6] Ibid., p. 72.

[7] Cf., David Hume, An Inquiry Concerning Human Understanding, ed. by Charles W. Hendel (New York: Liberal Arts Press, 1955), ch. 7.

[8] Ibid., p. 87.

[9] Grammar of Assent, p. 70.

[10] David Hume, op. cit., p. 79.

[11] Grammar of Assent, p. 71.

[12] James Collins, Philosophical Readings in Cardinal Newman (Chicago: Henry Regnery Co. 1961). pp. 195-196.

[13] John Henry Newman, The Idea of a University (Garden City, N.Y.: Image Books, Doubeday and Co., Inc., 1959), pp. 78-79.

[14] I. Kant, Critique of Pure Reason, tr. by Norman Kemp Smith (New York: 1950), pp. 518 ff.

[15] John Henry Newman, op. cit., pp. 76-77.

[16] Grammar of Assent, p. 52.

[17] _Ibid._, p. 90.

[18] _Ibid._, p. 97.

[19] _Ibid._, p. 93.

[20] _Ibid._, p. 96.

[21] Cf., _The Argument from Conscience to the Existence of God_, A. Boekraad and H. Tristam, Nauwelaerts, Louvain, 1961, ch. IV.

[22] _Grammar of Assent_, p. 99.

[23] _Ibid._

[24] _Grammar of Assent_, pp. 100 ff.

[25] _Ibid._

[26] _Ibid._, p. 101.

[27] _Ibid._, p. 102.

[28] _Ibid._, p. 305.

[29] _Ibid._, pp. 305-306.

[30] _The Argument from Conscience to the Existence of God_, pp. 118-119.

[31] _Grammar of Assent_, p. 136.

[32] _Ibid._, p. 217.

[33] _Ibid._, p. 230.

[34] _Ibid._, pp. 234-239.

[35] _Ibid._, p. 240.

[36] _Ibid._, p. 250.

[37] _Ibid._

[38]Ibid., p. 251.

[39]Ibid., p. 254.

[40]Ibid.

[41]Ibid., p. 270.

[42]Ibid., p. 271.

[43]Ibid., pp. 274-275

[44]Ibid., p. 279.

[45]Ibid., p. 280.

[46]The Idea of a University, p. 203.

[47]Ibid., p. 204.

II

SØREN KIERKEGAARD

Søren Kierkegaard was born in 1813 and died in 1855. His life spans only about half the time as Newman's and there is no evidence that either was aware of the other. Yet there are striking similarities in their individual approaches to God. Like Newman, Kierkegaard made Christianity a deep concern of the individual conscience and no one was more aware of the need for each man to be alone before God. His stress is always on the subject and the individual, and he fought constantly any approach to religion and to God that absorbed the individual into the mass, that exalted the universal over the particular, that "systematized" salvation, or made it equivalent to a set of objective rules that would automatically at the proper time produce its effect. His rejection of all such objectivizing man's relationship to truth and to God has rightly made him, if not the founder, at least one of the principal sources of contemporary existentialism. There is much in the work of Kierkegaard that has had a profound influence on such different authors as Heidegger, Jaspers, Sartre, Marcel, and Tillich. Kierkegaard's insistence on the subjective and the singular brought him into immediate conflict with most of the accepted philosophical and religious thinking of his day.

THE REJECTION OF HEGEL

The predominant philosophical thought of the nineteenth century was that of the German philosopher, G. W. F. Hegel. According to Hegel, finite reality was nothing else but a temporal extrapolation of the Absolute Mind striving to achieve a realization of itself. The Absolute—Being—was at one and the same time both everything and nothing. For from one aspect Being is absolutely all-inclusive containing every richness and all perfection. From another, Being is the lowest possible common denominator of all things, the poorest element in reality, undetermined and unspecified. From this aspect Being corresponds to nothing, for every-

thing that exists is always something determinate and
specific. It is from this basic contradiction at the
heart of the concept of Being that Becoming proceeds
and an eternal process is set in motion. Thus the
Absolute Mind thinks itself and all things, thinks itself in all things and through all things, coming to an
ever more perfect understanding of what is entailed in
Absolute Mind. Man, to take only one example, is the
Absolute thinking itself in each individual man. Thus
the "System" becomes increasingly more perfect insofar
as it becomes ever more abstract and universal, encom-
passing within itself an evermore complete and univer-
salized expression of itself.

        Hegel, furthermore, saw Christianity as a more
or less imaginative expression of what he was saying
philosophically. In other words, as Hegel saw it,
Christianity, too, would ultimately be absorbed in the
"System". Kierkegaard, however, would have none of it.
His rejection of Hegel is both philosophical and religious. He attacked Hegel where he is most vulnerable.
It is not the universal but the individual which is
most important. An eternal, objective dialectic into
which the individual has been made a temporary means to
an impersonal end can never replace the personal search
for personal truth. Such a dialectic swallows up the
finite and the individual person. But for every human
being his personal existence as a subject is much more
real than is any objective impersonal process. If there
is truth to be found, the individual must take it into
his own personal subjective existence and give it a real
existential mode in the world. Pure thought can never
become real, for it is always abstract. But the human
person is real and can be the realizing factor for a
truth achieved by the subject and expressed in his life.
Unless Christianity is a truth so attained and so expressed, it is falsified. Kierkegaard's rejection of
Hegel, then, is based on his realization that the existence of the individual as a subject is more important
than is any universal and that subjectivity is essential
to the realization of Christian truth.

REJECTION OF A SECULARIZED CHRISTIANITY
        Kierkegaard rejected the Hegelian dialectic be-
cause it took place entirely on an abstract, universal

level and swallowed up the singular and the individual person. His objection to the secularized Christianity of his time is that the dialectic in this area has been reduced entirely to the finite level. Kierkegaard was convinced that Christianity as practiced by the mass of people in Denmark had lost nearly all of its other-worldly quality and had been reduced to mere "playing at Christianity". Christianity had been reduced to lip service and convenience. It was a "Sunday Christianity" with little realization of the real commitment demanded by the Gospels. It was a Christianity without passion and with little use for suffering and the imitation of Christ.

Neither were the clergy nor even Luther himself exempt from Kierkegaard's attack. He saw them as the ones most responsible for the watered down version of the Christianity most people were practicing, and seriously questioned whether a clergyman could be a real Christian. Kierkegaard himself had refused orders, and even went so far as to refuse the sacrament from a clergyman on his deathbed. His criticism of Bishop Mynster is well known.

Now he is dead. It would have been most desirable if he could have been persuaded to end his life by confessing to Christianity that what he represented was not really Christianity, but a milder form of it; for he supported a whole generation. . . . Now that he is dead without having made it, everything is changed; all that is left is that by his preaching he has hardened Christianity into a deception.[1]

Christianity must be led back to the monastery from which Luther broke out. The trouble with the monastic life was not the asceticism nor the celibacy. On the contrary, these are elements of a vital and dedicated Christianity. The difficulty is that life in a monastery has come to be regarded as an extraordinary practice of Christianity, while that practiced by people in the world had come to be considered ordinary and sufficient.

No, asceticism and all that belongs to it is merely a first thing: it is a condition for being able to be a witness to the truth.

31

So the turn which Luther brought about was a mistake: it was not a reduction but a raising that was required.[2]

Kierkegaard sees, too, in Lutheranism an exaggerated emphasis on faith to the detriment of works, at least as this was superficially understood in Denmark. Luther arrived at his principle of the utter necessity of faith as a beginning only after long years of struggle and deep concern. But works are the ordinary beginning and were so even for Luther. We do judge a man by his works. It does little good for a worldly, superficial Christian to proclaim that in his heart he is really and thoroughly dedicated to the Christian way of life. A man's deeds are an expression of himself and of his values. Faith may be impossible except as a pure gift of God, but there must be something given by the individual, too, as a sign of his willingness and his commitment.

> The moment I mention 'works' one thinks at once of Catholicism. So as not to be misunderstood, I will remark (although it does not need--or in any case, ought not to need--remarking) that naturally everything Catholicism has hit upon in connection with the meritoriness of works is unconditionally to be rejected. But on the heels of that I say that the works-principle is simpler than the faith-principle. And why? Because the works-princple begins with the beginning and begins with that which is common to us men; the principle of faith begins so far forward that in every generation there are not many who get that far. Hence this principle becomes perfectly meaningless when people will begin with it without further ado.[3]

The situation, then, as Kierkegaard saw it, was this. Men were dissipating themselves in Hegelian abstractions, in an unreal rationalism, and in a pseudo, watered down Christianity. It was a drifting state provided with well-worm chichés that made everything seem all right but what was really a sickness unto death. It was from this sickness that Kierkegaard hoped to cure the society of his time. That cure involved the re-introduction of a thoroughgoing Christianity which was so intense that it may well be true that only Christ Himself ever was able to practice it. At any rate, Kierkegaard re-

garded his mission as that of introducing Christianity
into Christendom. He was well aware that the ideal he
proposed was a sublime one. He knew, too, that few men,
including himself, would ever attain more than a partial share in it. But he remained entirely convinced
that the attempt had to be made by each man, freely and
existentially, if he were to become what he was meant
to be.

THE NATURE OF THE SELF

Kierkegaard is not interested in speaking about
man in the abstract, Hegelian sense. It is the existing individual who is important and not some universal
definition. When he defines, or describes, the individual, then, he does so in terms that will explain not
only the individual's infinite possibilities but also
the inadequacies that seem to dog his every step in his
existence in the world. Man, says Kierkegaard in The
Sickness Unto Death, is a spirit, and a spirit is a
self. But what is a self? The self is a relation
which relates itself to its own self. To say it another
way, man is a composite of soul and body and spirit.
Soul and body are naturally related to each other.
Spirit is there as self insofar as it enables an individual to become consciously aware of what he is, and
also to make each one aware that he is related beyond
himself to another.

Such a derived, constituted relation is the human
self, a relation which relates itself to its own
self, and in relating itself to its own self, relates itself to another.[4]

A maturely constituted self, then, is an individual who
is aware that he is spirit and matter and that he has
been so structured by God upon Whom he is dependent and
without Whom he can never attain nor maintain the equilibrium and rest which is necessary for him to progress
toward what he is meant to be.

Such a composition of spirit and matter, however,
is not a single thing. The synthesis implies within itself a profound complexity, when it is considered from
different aspects. For spirit and matter signify also
a synthesis of the infinite and the finite, of the

33

eternal and the temporal, of freedom and necessity.
This synthesis, grounded in consciousness and related
to God, is the existing individual who is called upon
to live in awareness before God and to bring to fulfillment at least some of the potentialities which his
synthetic nature makes possible.

That this is not an easy task is readily understandable. Exaggeration of one or the other element is
always possible. Such exaggeration, a commitment to one
side of the synthesis or the other, results in despair
of ever achieving the equilibrium which nature itself
demands. One can become absorbed in the infinite to
the detriment of the finite, in necessity to the ex-
clusion of freedom, in the temporal and forget the
eternal. One can even become unaware of one or the
other of the opposing aspects and not even know that he
is condemning himself to an unnatural and despairing
situation. Despair is a dis-relationship, a sickness
in the synthetic nature of the individual, which, if
not controlled, will lead him to destruction.

When such a condition is deliberately willed or
consented to before God, that is, with awareness of God,
then this despair is called sin. For sin is nothing
else but the refusal to be before God what God wants me
to be. On the other hand, the opposite of this is
called faith. For "Faith is: that the self in being
itself and in willing to be itself is grounded trans-
parently in God".[5] There are other forms of sin, but
basically it always consists in a rejection of faith.
As we shall see, the individual can only find his fulfillment, can only achieve his selfhood, in turning
toward a truth to which he must existentially dedicate
himself; that is, a truth which he must live, grounded
in faith, though it be beyond the grasp of finite reason.

SUBJECTIVITY
This human individual so constructed, but incomplete, is ordered to become himself and is given the
possibility of eternal blessedness. But the latter possibility is entirely dependent on the actuality of the
former. Only by becoming what he is can he eventually
become what he is meant to be. Now each individual is

34

an existing subject, and it must be that only in the development of his personal subjectivity does he ever achieve himself. Kierkegaard does not use subjectivity in the sense that there are no objects, or that only subjects exist. He is very well aware of objectivity. He simply does not want objectivity so to rule the world of men that it destroys what each man is in his own essence.

It will help here to consider his criticism of what is ordinarily known as objective truth.[6] Objective truth, he tells us, can be taken in two ways. One can understand the term empirically, and then it means the correspondence between thought and being. Here the difficulty will be that neither the thinker nor the empirical being under consideration is completed. Each is still in process, and truth is bound to remain open at both ends. If, on the other hand, one takes truth to mean the correspondence between being and thought on the idealistic or abstract level, then truth becomes merely a tautology. In either case, also, the individual is more and more swallowed up by the object until he simply vanishes. He is always on the outside and becomes less and less important as the truth in question becomes more and more so. This is precisely the sort of truth that one runs into in the sciences, in history, in rationalistic philosophy. The only reason that the individual does not vanish completely and become absolutely identified with the object under study is that he happens to be a subject existing in time, whether he likes it or not.

The subjective reflection turns its attention inwardly to the subject, and desires in this intensification of inwardness to realize the truth. And it proceeds in such fashion that, just as in the preceding objective reflection, when the objectivity had come into being, the subjectivity had vanished, so here the subjectivity of the subject becomes the final stage, and objectivity a vanishing factor.[7]

Kierkegaard further insists that all essential knowledge relates to existence, and what does not relate to existence is not essential knowledge. But he does not mean by this the identity which abstract thought postulates between thought and being. He means knowledge that has a relationship to the knower who is essentially an existing individual. In other words, the only real essential knowledge, or, perhaps, knowledge which it is necessary for the individual to possess, is that which will affect the individual in such a way as to bring him closer to completion as the total human person he is. This sort of knowledge will make a difference, will involve passion and emotion as well as intellect, and will demand choice and commitment. The conclusion which Kierkegaard draws is evident: only ethical and ethico-religious knowledge has an essential relationship to the existence of the knower.

What is important in the grasp of truth in subjectivity is the way it is achieved rather than what is achieved. If this mode is correct, then the individual is in the truth, even if he should be (accidentally) related to what is not true. Here Kierkegaard uses the knowledge of God as an example. Objectively one can ask whether the object in question is in fact the true God. Subjectively the question becomes whether the individual is related to something in such a manner that the relationship is in truth a God-relationship. Thus, for example, the man who worships an idol with passion and sincerity and allows this relationship to become a directing influence in his life may very well be in a better position than one who prays formally to the true God, but who has no real idea of what God is or who does not allow the God-concept to affect his life in any way at all.

Here we get some idea of Kierkegaard's lack of concern with philosophical proofs for the existence of God. The individual who chooses to pursue such a path to God enters upon a process which is at best approximative. Reason searches to bring God to light objectively. But this is eternally impossible, for God is a Subject, and God exists and is approachable only subjectively and in inwardness. The objective approach to God always leaves the inquirer with the vague apprehension that the God he finds may very well be only the creation of his own concepts. Besides the process is a long one, and the person who chooses the subjective way to God can find Him in an instant by virtue of the infinite passion of inwardness. Such a person recognizes

that the long objective process is not worth the time,
since every moment is wasted in which one does not
have God.

In this manner God certainly becomes a postulate,
but not in the otiose manner in which the word is
commonly understood. It becomes clear rather that
the only way in which an existing individual comes
into relation with God, is when the dialecical
contradiction brings his passion to the point of
despair, and helps him to embrace God with the
'category of despair' (faith). Then the postulate
is so far from being arbitrary that it is precisely
a life-necessity. It is then not so much that God
is a postulate, as that the existing individual's
postulation of God is a necessity.[8]

At this point, if one were to ask on which side there is
the most truth, whether on the side of the one who seeks
the true God objectively, and who pursues the approxi-
mate truth of the God-idea; or on the side of the one
who, driven by the passion of his need for God, feels
an infinite concern for his own relationship to God in
truth, the answer must be quite clear to anyone who has
not been demoralized with the aid of science.

This subjective grasping of the truth includes
further a radical freedom as part of the very nature of
the individual. There is a striving here, a passion,
which only the individual can specify, for the intellect
is not determined in such a case by the clarity of the
object. To put it another way, the objective evidence
in the case is not such as to force the intellect to a
philosophical conclusion. There may be order in the
world, but there is disorder, too. There is good, but
there is also evil. The intellect may face the uncertainty and be held fast forever. If the existing individual is to achieve the truth, there is necessity here
for a leap, a freely made decision helped by passion to
reach out to the truth before which reason alone would
stand in abeyance. In such a situation Kierkegaard is
willing to define truth as "an objective uncertainty
held fast in an appropriation-process of the most passionate inwardness".[9] Hence, truth becomes a venture,
a risk, an uncertainty on which the individual is willing

to stake everything. As we shall see, this is precisely the point where faith may enter in.

Subjectivity, then, for Kierkegaard is not idealistic. It is rather a turning away from abstraction
and rationalism to the self which really exists in a
real situation. It does not deny the possibility of
objective knowledge or truth, but it insists that the
essential knowledge for any person is always a knowledge which deeply concerns his own personal existence.
Such a knowledge would be concerned with what it means
to be an I, with death as a reality for me, with sin
and guilt, with the possibility of God, with the future,
and with my own completion in that future. Such a reflective inwardness brings me face to face with uncertainty and paradox. It presupposes, therefore, a radical freedom at the heart of each man. And that freedom
is to be specified and determined by the individual in
his own existential situation. How it is done is in
the long run more important for his own authenticity
than what is done. But Kierkegaard is also sure that,
if the how is wrong, this, too, will be manifested in
the working out of it.

Such subjectivity results, furthermore, in a
passionate reaching out to truths that I as an individual need to complete myself. These are no abstract
formulations of truth, but truths which will enter into
my life and my activity. They involve commitment and
dedication, a day to day awareness of the extent to
which they are measuring my actions. There is an isolation involved in this, to be sure. Only the individual
can and must make the decisions that affect him. No
one else, much less a group, could possibly do it for
him. But the isolation is never complete. The freedom
involved in this inward awareness offers an escape from
the circle of immanence which rationalism or the System
would make impossible. Precisely because of the uncertainty in the paradoxical situation, there is room for
an "I will," or an "I choose," and every authentic choice
brings the individual another step nearer to what it
means to be a self.

The road to such subjectivity is a difficult one,
however. It has its dark side as well as its hope. It

may offer the possibility of transcendence, but the path may well lead through the depths of despair.

DREAD

In **The Concept of Dread**[10] Kierkegaard traces the psychological path which man pursues on the natural level toward the possibility of salvific faith. In the beginning each man is innocent, but this innocence is also an ignorance. He is a composition of soul and body and spirit. But the spirit is dreaming; it is not yet awakened. The individual is in an immediate relationship with his environment, but he is also as yet unaware of his possibilities. What are these possibilities? He does not know. He is prevented by spirit from sinking into the immediacy of the animal level. He is also not yet subjectively aware of what it means to be spirit. In his innocence he is also ignorant of I-know-not-what. This I-know-not-what is for the individual a nothingness. This nothingness is precisely the object of dread.

An example may help here. When Adam is commanded by God not to eat of the tree of good and evil under pain of death, he still has no idea of what this means. But the prohibition alarms Adam because it awakens in him the possibility of Freedom. His innocence gives way to a state of apprehension, of being able; but it is still not clear of what he is capable.

What it is he is able to do, of that he has no conception; to suppose that he had some conception is to suppose, as commonly is done, what came later, the distinction between good and evil. There is only the possibility of being able, as a higher form of ignorance, as a heightened expression of dread, because this in a more profound sense is and is not, because in a more profound sense he loves it and flees from it.[11]

Dread, then, is an awakening realization of freedom pointing toward possibility, but what the possibility is is as yet unknown. Adam soon found out at least one aspect of what the possibility of freedom implied. And so each man finds it out when he freely constitutes himself in his own guilt as modified and intensified by

39

the guilt of the race. For Adam's sin is there always,
objectively, adding to the significance of a creation
founded in innocence. This is what Kierkegaard calls
objective dread.[12]

SUBJECTIVE DREAD
        In speaking of dread in the individual, Kierke-
gaard likens it to a dizziness. If one chances to look
down into a yawning abyss, he becomes dizzy. But the
reason for the dizziness is as much in the eye as it is
in the abyss. So dread is the dizziness of freedom
which occurs when the spirit in man would attempt to
synthesize and bring to fulfillment the disparate elements of soul and body. Spirit, aware of its own freedom and its possibility, reaches out to the finite to
sustain itself, and in doing so succumbs. When freedom
arises again, it sees that it is guilty. Between these
two instants lies the leap which no science has explained or can explain. It is the leap into sin. This
leap is always an act of the individual. He may well
bear the burden of the guilt of the race, but his own
determination of his freedom in the face of his own
possibility always remains his and his alone. Sin has
been called an egoism, and in this Kierkegaard finds
another reason why such an act cannot be handled by
science. As we shall see, the saving act is just as
personal.

    Seeing that in modern philosophy sin has so often
    been explained as egoism, it is incomprehensible
    that no one has perceived that precisely in this
    consists the impossibility of finding a place for
    sin in any science. For the egoistic is precisely
    the particular (Enkelte), and only the particular
    individual can know it, as a particular individual,
    since when viewed under general categories it can
    signify everything, in such wise that this every-
    thing signifies nothing at all. Therefore the defi-
    nition of sin as egoism may be quite correct, pre-
    cisely when at the same time one holds fast the fact
    that, scientifically speaking, it is so empty of
    content that it means nothing at all.[13]

        Kierkegaard has defined man as a composition of
soul and body made aware of itself and the possibility

of transcendence by spirit. In relation to dread man
is also described as a composition of the temporal and
the eternal. He is able to do this because the spirit
in man looks toward the future and the future is identifiable with the eternal. We speak, for example, of
eternal life as a future life. But the spirit in man
also makes it possible for man to bring the eternal in
an instant into the temporal orbit in which the individual is also immersed. Reality is really a present instant looking toward the future. From this viewpoint
the past is unreal. Hence, just as spirit looks toward
the future in this instant; so, too, does dread involve
the unknown possibility which will be determined by freedom in an instant. But the individual is also concerned
with the material and the temporal. This necessarily
concerns the sensuous element in man. Sensuousness is
not sin any more than freedom is virtue. But sensuousness can become sin by reason of sin just as freedom
can be made virtuous by reason of spirit. But in the
instant, before the determination is made, dread arises
as a dizzying possibility of freedom. If freedom succumbs to the temporal and the sensuous, it also in that
instant rejects the spiritual and the eternal. Sin is
the capitulation to matter, to sensousness, and to time.
It determines freedom to what it dreaded--the possibility
of freedom's misuse. As spirit it rejects itself. It
is because of this that guilt arises and remains in relation to future possibilities.

> Dread is the psychological state which precedes sin,
> comes as near as possible to it, and is as provoca-
> tive as possible of dread, but without explaining
> sin, which breaks forth first in the qualitative
> leap. The instant sin is posited, the temporal is
> sin. We do not say that the temporal is sinfulness,
> any more than that the sensuous is sinfulness; but
> for the fact that sin is posited the temporal sig-
> nifies sinfulness. Therefore that man sins who
> lives merely in the instant abstracted from the
> eternal.[14]

Here again the emphasis is put on the individual,
the subject. There is no such thing for Kierkegaard as
freedom in the abstract. The determination of the self
in an instant with regard to the future always takes

place in the concrete. In that instant each individual
identifies himself as it were, in relation to the elements which make him himself--soul, matter, and spirit.
Dread resolves itself momentarily, at least, in guilt,
repentance, or salvation. Should it resolve itself as
sin, then the object of dread, previously a nothingness,
now becomes really something. This state can continue
and intensify itself, until sin itself becomes the
actuality and the determination toward good the possibility. In this case dread arises in the face of good as
a present nothingness and an unknown. This is the de-
moniacal, that terrible situation where an individual
flees the eternal and the spiritual in preference for
the sensuous and the temporal.

THE POSITIVE SIDE OF DREAD

Because dread is the possibility of freedom, it
can become absolutely educative. For it can, with the
aid of faith, see through all finite aims and discover
all their deceptions.[15] The possibility of which Kierkegaard speaks here is not that which is commonly understood; the possibility, for example, of luck or good
fortune. It is that knowledge which a man has that he
can demand of life absolutely nothing, that every unknown terror may become fact in the next instant. This
knowledge gives a man an entirely different outlook on
life and reality. Thus, possibility becomes a heavier
burden to bear than the actual, and whatever he is
called upon to bear actually will remain far lighter
than the possibility ever is. It is in this way that
the individual truly learns the difference between the
infinite and the finite.

But in order that the individual may thus absolutely
and infinitely be educated by possibility, he must
be honest toward possibility and must have faith. By
faith, I mean what Hegel in his fashion calls very
rightly 'the inward certainty which anticiapates infinity.' When the discoveries of possibility are
honestly administered, possibility will then dis-
close all finitudes but idealize them in the form of
infinity, and by dread overwhelm the individual, until he in turn conquers them by the anticipation of
faith.[16]

The alternative is to turn away from possibility and to
settle for the finite and the known. It is to grapple
with the daily categories of the reasonable and the
commonplace. This, however, is to sink ever more deeply
into the actual. It is to turn away from faith as that
which is unreasonable and too demanding from a human
standpoint. Men ordinarily think that true education
consists in being concerned in crises, in being joined
with someone who performs heroic feats, in knowing which
way the world is going and in having a hand in deter-
mining its course. But all this is a flight from possibility and from infinity. The door is closed in upon
the self, and the stifling process begins. Faith is no
longer even a possibility. Such a man is lost.

SAVING FAITH

The man who has truly learned from dread, conceived as the possibility of freedom, at least remains
open to the infinite, to a dialogue with the infinite
instead of to a dialogue which concerns itself only with
finite categories and temporal goals. But Kierkegaard
warns the reader to make no mistake about what he means
here. This dialogue with the infinite has its own difficulties, and the faith that is required to pursue it
is totally unlike a rationalistic approach to truth. In
The Philosophical Fragments[17] he tries to establish a
clear difference between the way Socrates discovered
truth and the way a Christian discovers it. The contrast is made between Socrates as teacher and Christ as
Teacher and Savior. According to Socrates, one cannot
even begin the search for truth, unless, somehow, he has
an idea of what he is searching for. Hence, the task of
the teacher is to awaken the pupil to the truth which he
already possesses within himself. This is the whole
Platonic doctrine of recollection. That is why Socrates
never claimed to be anything but a mid-wife. The individual may need to enter into a relationship with another in order to make his quest for truth fruitful, but he
himself must ultimately undergo the labor of producing
the truth out of himself. The teacher is at best an
occasion, an historical accident, who must fade out of
the picture once the pupil is able to advance on his own.

It was thus Socrates understood himself, and thus he
thought that everyone must understand himself, in

43

the light of this understanding interpreting his
relationship to each individual, with equal humility
and with equal pride. He had the courage and self-
possession to be sufficient unto himself, but also
in his relations to his fellowmen to be merely an
occasion, even when dealing with the meanest capacity.
How rare is such magnanimity![18]

The situation is quite different, however, if we
suppose that the seeker does not possess the truth within himself but must receive it from outside. In this
case the seeker after a truth which he does not possess
is in a state of error. Up to this point the Socratic
approach is valid, for only the individual can become
cognizant of his own error. But once this happens, the
situation changes radically. For if the truth is to
come from outside, and if the present condition of the
learner is one of error, then the teacher must not only
bring the truth to the learner, but also the condition
which makes it possible to receive it. The very nature
of the learner must be re-constituted, so to speak, by
the teacher. The teacher must make himself present to
the learner, on the learner's level, historically; but,
and much more importantly, as possessing a communicable
truth which the learner of his own accord could never
achieve. This is precisely what the God-Man has done
and continues to do with everyone who sincerely seeks Him.

But when the God becomes a Teacher, his love cannot
be merely seconding and assisting, but is creative,
giving a new being to the learner, or as we have
called him, the man born anew; by which designation
we signify the transition from non-being to being.
The truth then is that the learner owes the Teacher
everything. But this is what makes it so difficult to
effect an understanding: that the learner becomes as
nothing and yet is not destroyed; that he comes to
owe everything to the Teacher and yet retains his confidence; that he understands the Truth and yet that
the Truth makes him free; that he apprehends the guilt
of his Error and yet that his confidence rises victori-
ous in the Truth. Between man and man the Socratic
mid-wifery is the highest relation, a begetting is reserved for the God, whose love is <u>creative</u>, but not
merely in the sense which Socrates so beautifully ex-
pounds on a certain festal occasion.[19]

Well and good. But at this point reason comes into violent collision with the basic paradox of the whole situation. The teacher who offers his truth is the God-Man. He is the Eternal immersed in time, the Infinite in finite garb, the Absolutely Different Who is like the learner. He is the Unlimited in Whose presence reason reaches its own limit and disperses itself. Nor could reason ever prove that such a Being ever existed.

> The idea of demonstrating that this unknown something (the God) exists, could scarcely suggest itself to the Reason. For if the God does not exist it would of course be impossible to prove it; and if he does exist it would be folly to attempt it.[20]

DIFFICULTY OF PROOF OF GOD'S EXISTENCE

It seems to me that Kierkegaard merges two different questions here. At least it is not always clear whether he is talking about the impossibility of proving that Christ is God or whether he is saying that it is equally impossible to prove that God exists. The first is evident enough, if one accepts his contention that the Divine Teacher must Himself produce in the learner the condition which makes it possible for the learner to accept the Teacher as Divine. This is common Christian dogma. On the other hand, if he is saying that it is impossible to prove that there exists a Being Whom we call God, an ultimate and infinite source of all things, this is something else again. He does seem to be saying both, and his rejection of the proof for the existence of God is obviously based on the inadequacy of the ontological argument, expecially as it was formulated by Spinoza.

> But if when I speak of proving the God's existence I mean that I propose to prove that the Unknown, which exists, is God, then I express myself unfortunately. For in that case I do not prove anything, least of all an existence, but merely develop the content of a conception.[21]

Kierkegaard thinks that it is difficult enough to prove that anything exists. Proof always moves from existence not toward existence. We do not prove, for

45

example, that a stone exists, but that something which exists is a stone. A court of law does not prove that a criminal exists, but that the accused, whose existence is given, is a criminal. Even if I were to proceed from the deeds of God to the existence of God, who is to say what are the deeds of God? I would have to pre-suppose this to begin with, but what is this but to pre-suppose that God exists? One is reminded of Newman here and his statement that he accepted finality in the uni-verse because he believed in God; he did not believe in God because of finality in the universe.

Kierkegaard's position is that the demonstration for God's existence always involves a leap. And this is certainly true if the proof used is the ontological argu-ment. There is no other way to get existence out of essence, to derive reality from the possibility of the concept. There are other considerations, too, which in-dicate that it is impossible for reason to approach God. Reason comes into collision with the Unknown. This Un-known exists, but insofar as it is Unknown, it does not exist. Thus, this Unknown becomes a limit and a tor-ment for reason, and yet reason can go no further. This Unknown is, moreover, the absolutely different and rea-son cannot even conceive an absolute unlikeness. The reason cannot negate itself absolutely, but uses itself for the purpose, and thus conceives only such an unlike-ness within itself as it can conceive by means of itself. It cannot absolutely transcend itself, and hence con-ceives only such a superiority over itself as it can conceive by means of itself. Reason then remains at the limit, tormented, baffled, and impotent.

But the paradox becomes still more intense.

From this there would seem to follow the further con-sequence, that if man is to receive any true know-ledge about the Unknown (the God) he must be made to know that it is unlike him, absolutely unlike him. This knowledge the Reason cannot possibly obtain of itself; we have already seen that this would be a self contradiction. It will therefore have to ob-tain this knowledge from the God. But even if it obtains such knowledge it cannot understand it, and thus is quite unable to possess such knowledge. For

46

how should the Reason be able to understand what is
absolutely different from itself? . . . For if the
God is absolutely unlike man, then man is absolutely
unlike the God; but how could reason be expected to
understand this? Here we seem to be confronted with
a paradox. Merely to obtain the knowledge that the
God is unlike him, man needs the help of the God;
and now he learns that the God is absolutely different from himself. But if the God and man are absolutely different, this cannot be accounted for on
the basis of what man derives from the God, for in
so far they are akin. Their unlikeness must therefore be explained by what man derives from himself
. . . .22

And here Kierkegaard suggests a possible way out of the
seeming contradiction. What man derives from himself
and which makes him totally unlike God is sin, which
was previously called error. If the God-Man, the Teacher, chooses to make himself like man in all things save
sin, it is to lead him out of sin and error to a likeness with the Totally Other, the Unknown God. Reason
may still boggle at this, but there is an analogy, imperfect though it be, presented by love. For reason to
assent to the paradox would seem to suggest its own
downfall. But this is precisely what love does.

Self-love lies at the ground of love; but the paradoxical passion of self-love when at its highest
pitch wills precisely its own downfall. This is also
what love desires, so that these two are linked in
mutual understanding in the passion of the moment,
and this passion is love. Why should not the lover
find this conceivable? But he who in self-love
shrinks from the touch of love can neither understand
it nor summon the courage to venture it, since it
means his downfall. Such is then the passion of
love; self-love is indeed submerged but not annihi-
lated; it is taken captive and becomes love's spolia
opima. . . .23

     If natural reason, then, when confronted with the
paradox of the God-Man, the Eternal in time, will surrender itself to the Unknown God, the Redeemer who provides the condition for redemption, it will have seized

for itself in that moment the beginning of its salvation. If, on the contrary, this moment becomes a scandal to it, an offense to reason because it--the paradox--
is seemingly absurd, then reason sinks back into itself.
The moment of choice becomes a stumbling block, a folly,
and the possibility of likeness to the Unknown God is
shut off by the reason's rejection of the offered possibility. This moment, in other words, is what Kierkegaard means by Faith. Only the man who can make such
an assent is able to transcend his finitude, his error,
his sin to that other realm in which he can become truly
what he has never been. But the ability to attain such
truth must itself be given by the Teacher if the assent
itself is to become actual. And more than this. The
Socratic teacher fades into the background as the learner turns more and more into himself to the truth which
was always immanent to him and which he has been helped
to recollect. Here, however, the Teacher, the God-Man,
remains predominant, and the assent is made to Him first
and foremost rather than to a truth expressed in formal
propositions or in a later developed "theory of salvation". It is only through the Christian commitment to
the God-Man, made possible by the gift of faith, which
the God-Man Himself must provide, that Kierkegaard sees
for man a point of departure to eternal Truth and
eternal fulfillment.

THE PARADOX AND THE ABSURD
        Kierkegaard in his association of Christianity
with paradox has been accused of associating it also
with irrationalism. Must a man really give up his reason to be a Christian? Does he really assent to absurdity when he makes an act of faith? To say that some of
his language is not always clear on the point is truly
an understatement, but in the long run it is difficult
to maintain the position that he did associate Christianity and absurdity. It seems much more correct to
say that he was drawing a contrast between the act of
faith in the God-Man and the complete abstract rationalism of the Hegelian system, which theoretically would
explain everything. He also makes a distinction between
the suave philosophical reasoning of Climacus, who is
not a Christian, and the real Christian assent to re
vealed mystery. Climacus, for example, can appreciate
Christianity as a world view, but he cannot bring him-

self to make the personal existential act that will commit him to a lived acceptance of the Christian way of life. Reason hesitates at the brink because it is faced with an objective uncertainty, a mystery, and can make of the uncertainty a scandal and an offense to reason. The rationalistic system, for which all things are ultimately explicable, will also take offense at the assertion that reason's highest achievement must be to negate itself in the face of what is in essence not understandable. Hence the paradox, the mystery of the God-Man, the union of the temporal and the Eternal, which is the basic doctrine of Christianity, can be an affront to natural and philosophic reason.

The man who becomes aware of his personal individuality and of his relationship to God; who has faced despair and dread; who has been taught by the infinite possibility of his own dependence and insignificance; who is trying to live in utter transparency before God; this man is brought into confrontation with the only real possibility of transcendence and salvation; a certain man, Jesus Christ, is truly God and is the only answer to despair and sin. At this point such an individual must make a profoundly subjective act of assent and acceptance of the situation or must turn away from what he considers to be an offense to his reason and, therefore, impossible to accept. For the man who turns away the Paradox is, indeed, absurd. But for the man who under grace can make the assent, the Paradox is seen as truly acceptable, even though he cannot understand how such a thing is possible. In a statement in his _Journals_ Kierkegaard says that the Absurd is merely a negative category. He agrees with Hugh of St. Victor that in the things which are above reason faith is not supported by reason because faith does not at all understand what it yet believes with all its power.

No, the concept of the absurd is strictly this: to understand that one cannot understand. A negative category, but as dialectical as all other positive categories. The absurd, the paradox is constructed in such a way that in fact reason could not by its own power reduce it to nonsense and show its emptiness. No; it is a sign, an enigma faced with which reason can only say: "I cannot resolve it; for me

that is not intelligible.' But it does not follow
therefrom that the paradox is in fact nonsense. But
we see that if we abolish faith completely reason
becomes presumptuous and will dare conclude 'ergo
the paradox is nonsense'. . . . Faith believes in
the Paradox, it believes the Paradox. Let us say
then, to quote Hugo de St. Victor's words that 'reason can well allow itself be determined to honour
faith' for it gains profundity by the negative category of the Paradox.[24]

And again later in the <u>Journals</u> Kierkegaard emphasizes that the Absurd about which he is talking is so
only for the third person, the outsider, who uses the
claim of absurdity to explain his rejection of the
Paradox.

The 'immediate' believer cannot apprehend the thought
that the content of faith is, for the reason and for
the third person who is not a believer, the absurd,
and that to become a believer everyone must be alone
with the absurd. . . . To understand that to the
reason it is the absurd, to speak of it thus quite
calmly to a third person, admitting that it is the
absurd, enduring the burden of the other man looking
upon it as the absurd--and nevertheless to believe it.
While naturally it is a matter of course that for
him who believes it is not the absurd.[25]

In the face of such texts it is difficult to accuse
Kierkegaard of identifying Christianity with irrationalism.

CHRISTIANITY AND SUBJECTIVITY
        On the other hand, this act of faith, which is
essentially an assent to the Paradox, does give Kierkegaard another chance to identify Christianity with subjectivity and, therefore, with the individual. He insists that Christianity has no objective existence in
the sense of an abstract philosophical system. Christianity either exists in an individual subject who em-
braces it, practices it, and is saved by it, or it does
not exist at all. This is not to deny that Christian
dogma can be expressed in propositions. But it does say
that as an existentialistic way of life it can only be
found in the existing individual.

The subjective acceptance is precisely the decisive factor; and an objective acceptance of Christianity (sit venia verbo) is paganism or thoughtlessness. Christianity proposes to endow the individual with an eternal happiness, a good which is not distributed wholesale, but only to one individual at a time. Though Christianity assumes that there inheres in the subjectivity of the individual, as being the potentiality of the appropriation of this good, the possibility of its acceptance, it does not assume that the subjectivity is immediately ready for such acceptance, or even has, without further ado, a real conception of the significance of such a good. The development of transformation of the individual's subjectivity, its infinite concentration in itself over against the conception of an eternal happiness, that highest good of the infinite--this constitutes the developed potentiality of the primary potentiality which subjectivity as such represents. In this way Christianity protests every form of objectivity: it desires that the subject should be infinitely concerned about himself. It is subjectivity that Christianity is concerned with, and it is only in subjectivity that its truth exists, if it exists at all; objectively, Christianity has absolutely no existence. If its truth happens to be only in a single subject, it exists in him alone; and there is greater Christian joy in heaven over this one individual than over universal history and the System, which as objective entities are incommensurable for that which is Christian.[26]

The philosophy of the age argues, on the contrary, that man's task is to become more and more objective. But again this is only abstract reason speaking. Christianity in its willingness to embrace truth and live it requires passion. But passion is subjectivity and does not exist objectively.

Not only is there in Christianity a triumph of the subjective over the objective, of the individual over the abstract, but there is also the vindication of the particular over the universal. If we go back to Abraham, who was also called upon to make an act of faith in the paradox of revelation, we see a concrete instance of this.

For Abraham's faith was, at least subjectively, no different from the one each Christian is called upon to make. In <u>Fear and Trembling</u> Kierkegaard discusses at length the dilemma with which Abraham was confronted when commanded by God to sacrifice his only son Isaac.[27] First of all, Abraham had to decide whether it really was a revealed command of God. In the second place the command seemed to contradict the promise, in which he had already believed against all hope, that he would be the father of many nations. In the third place the command seemed to violate the universal ethical law against murder. Which part of the revelation should Abraham believe? What right did he as an individual have to judge that he could perform an act which put him against the law of reason? How could he even know that he had received a revelation from God? Through page after page Kierkegaard graphically portrays the agony and uncertainty under which Abraham must surely have labored. Yet, when the decision had to be made, Abraham did not take offense. He believed without understanding, and truly became the "Father of all believers" when he set off with Isaac for Mount Moriah. He took a stand against the law that states: Murder is wrong, and against the advice he would have been given, had he consulted anyone. Abraham's act was truly an act of faith in a paradox, an assertion of his own individual faith against the universal and human reason.

So it must be with everyone who rises to an act of faith. And everyone who approaches faith is just as close to the object of that faith as was Abraham or any of the first disciples of Christ. The historical process has no influence whatever here. It is true that in the first century some people were privileged to see and associate with the historical Jesus, while those who came later must rely on historical testimony. But this is hardly the point where an act of faith is concerned which acknowledges Christ as the God-Man. If it is true that no one makes such an act without the immediate gift of grace from God Himself, then every Christian is on an equal footing and just as contemporary with Christ as were the first Apostles. For those who saw Him and associated with Him needed the gift of grace to accept Him as God as we do today. The Divinity was certainly not open to their eyes. They, too, faced the Paradox.

And just as there were those who believed in it, so, too, there were those who found it an offense and a scandal to reason and who turned away. Every man with the help of grace is able to take his stand with Peter and just as immediately say: "You are the Christ, the Son of the Living God". Thus faith becomes a second immediacy, just as natural, unreflective knowledge is the first. And on that second immediacy is built the whole attempt to become in truth a Christian.

CONCLUSION

It is admittedly difficult to evaluate Kierkegaard's contribution to contemporary thought. For a man who wanted no disciples and who was concerned lest the professors get hold of his works, he seems to have attracted a large enough crowd of both types. If one were to judge him by his stated mission of bringing Christianity back into Christendom, it would have to be said that he was not a notable success. He has been depicted as a lonely, half-mad figure, whose thought is difficult at best and at its worst disappears in confusion. As has been said, it would seem that only Christ could have practiced the kind of Christianity he urges upon the world. On the other hand, he is too dynamic, he has too many insights, both human and philosophical, to permit him to be dismissed as inconsequential. The interest that has grown up around him is indicative of that.

In the first place, his opposition to the Hegelian system has certainly borne fruit. The threat posed by abstract rationalism, especially in the areas of philosophy and science, has without doubt been modified by Kierkegaard's writing. His struggle to make the individual and not the system the primary area of concern has been difinitely successful. His stress on existence as opposed to essence and definition, has created a whole new philosophical approach centering around the individual as the real value in the universe. It is all very well to trace continental existentialism back to Socrates, but it remains true that contemporary existentialists owe much more to Kierkegaard than they do the to Greek philosopher. And however widely they may differ among themselves, however theistic or atheistic may be their varying conclusions, they are still dealing with Kierkegaard's basic themes. It is impossible to look at the writings

of any of the existentialists without meeting subjectivity, dread, the need for personal decision, the God
problem, the possibility of a personal ethics, the fact
of the self in a world of others, and a host of other
problems.

In the second place, from the Christian standpoint, Kierkegaard has drawn attention to the basic
nature of Christianity and its mission in the world. It
is not primarily a series of doctrines, although he never
denies that doctrine must be formulated. Nor can it consist in a lip service with which one gets involved only
for a stated time on a particular day of the week. If
Christianity has any meaning whatsoever, it must demand
a total commitment from the Christian for the living
out in his time and place of an ideal which is absolutely unique in history. It is this personal and existen-
tialized Christianity which Kierkegaard is so intensely
interested in distinguishing from the theoretical and
secularized Christianity that was everywhere apparent.
Philosophical proof was never intended in the Kierkegaardian dialectic to make one either a theist or a
Christian. God is there, revealing Himself through
Christ, and this God has to be faced by each man who has
heard of what has happened. To be what one is before
God, and not to despair ultimately of becoming what each
one is meant to be is the mark of the mature person.

But if one is to achieve such maturity, then a
return to subjectivity is absolutely essential. As we
have seen, this does not deny the possibility of trans-
subjective truth. But it does introduce the whole notion
of value into the struggle for truth, and the necessity
of a radical freedom at the heart of each man, if his
struggle to find and live the truth is to have any meaning. Kierkegaard never tires of insisting that a truth-
for-me is always more important than a truth-in-the abstract which never affects me personally. For the truth-
for-me gives rise to enthusiasm and passion, to a call
to work it out in the lived situation; and this, after
all, is the only meaningful human truth. If subjectivity
seems at times to be over-emphasized, it was the only way
Kierkegaard could find to combat that paralyzing objectivity that he thought had been foisted on men by the rationalism of Hegel. There is no implication, either, that the

attempt to achieve subjectivity is the easier way. On the contrary, the individual immediately exposes himself to the unknown possibility of the future, to anxiety and dread, to the need to understand how truth in the abstract must be applied to himself and lived out in practice. From this viewpoint error is very easily transformed into personal sin. Abstract knowledge comes to its limit when the question arises about the possibility of a redemption from that sin. From the viewpoint of the subject the means proposed may well appear to reason as an offense and a scandal; and the possibility of a subjectivity cut off from fulfillment, because it can "reasonably" commit itself no further may become an agonizing reality.

But it is also precisely because of such a possibility that Kierkegaard sees God as present to the world, and not exiled from it, as some later existentialists would have it. For the possibility of accepting the revealed hope of salvation, which may well look like an offense to finite reason, can never be actuated unless the God Who is present provides the means of acceptance. Hence, there is an immediate relationship between a revealing, sustaining God and the individual person trembling on the brink of his own possibility and freedom. It is the kind of a world most men have been taught exists. But it is also one in which the price for individual freedom and the relationship to a personal God is not bought cheaply. It is also a very human world in which the individual has a tremendous dignity along with his terrifying responsibility. Those who agonize over our present society where scientific technology threatens the very existence and meaning of the individual would do well to meditate on Kierkegaard's position.

It would be interesting also to consider what the man who was so critical of his society would have to say about ours. There is enough pseudo-Christianity, scepticism, and atheism about to provide him with a lot of material. The herd-man is still with us, and the drive for prestige and the "good" life based on having rather than being would be immediately recognized by him. He would have little use for a Christianity which has lost much of its respect for the Transcendent and the mysterious and which comes close to identifying itself with a somewhat pious and secular humanism.

His remarks on superficiality are also pertinent to a society whose manners and mores are more than a little dictated by advertising, convenience, and self-ishness. He might well be no more than a voice crying in the wilderness, but to the few who would listen that voice could prove very salvific.

Superficiality is the result of doing away with the vital distinction between concealment and manifesta-tion. It is the manifestation of emptiness, but where mere scope is concerned it wins, because it has the advantage of dazzling people with its bril-liant shams. Real manifestation is homogeneous, be-cause it is really profound, whereas superficiality has a varied and omnium gatherum appearance. Its love of showing off is the self-admiration of con-ceit in reflection. The concealment and reserve of inwardness is not given time in which to conceive an essential mystery, which can then be made manifest, but is disturbed long before that time comes and so, as a reward, reflection attracts the gaze of egotism upon its varied sham whenever possible.[28]

There are dozens of other areas where Kierkegaard's in-sight is as relevant today as it was in Denmark in 1845. He would much prefer that he be read and reflected upon by concerned individuals rather than interpreted and commented on by professors.

NOTES

NOTES

[1] *The Last Years, Journals*, 1853-1855, XI 1 A 1, ed. and tr. by Ronald Gregor Smith (New York: Harper and Row, 1975), p. 25.

[2] *Ibid.*, XI 1 A 134, p. 66.

[3] *Ibid.*, XI 2 A 301, p. 318.

[4] *The Sickness Unto Death*, tr. by Walter Lowrie (Princeton, N.J.: Princeton University Press, 1941), p. 18.

[5] *Ibid.*, p. 132.

[6] *Concluding Unscientific Postscript*, tr. by David Swenson, completed by Walter Lowrie (Princeton University Press, 1941), Cf. ch. 2.

[7] *Ibid.*, pp. 175-176.

[8] *Ibid.*, p. 179. Cf. footnote also.

[9] *Ibid.*, p. 182.

[10] *The Concept of Dread*, tr. by Walter Lowrie (Princeton, N.J.: Princeton University Press, 1957).

[11] *Ibid.*, p. 40.

[12] *Ibid.*, p. 52.

[13] *Ibid.*, p. 69.

[14] *Ibid.*, pp. 82-83.

[15] *Ibid.*, pp. 139 ff.

[16] *Ibid.*, pp. 140-141.

[17] *Philosophical Fragments*, tr. by David F. Swenson, Introduction and Commentary by Niels Thulstrup, revised and Commentary tr. by Howard V. Hong. (Princeton, N.J.: Princeton University Press, 1962).

[18] Ibid., p. 14

[19] Ibid., p. 38.

[20] Ibid., p. 49.

[21] Ibid.

[22] Ibid., pp. 57-58.

[23] Ibid., p. 59.

[24] Journals, X 2 A 354.

[25] Ibid., 1084.

[26] Postscript, p. 116.

[27] Fear and Trembling, tr. by Walter Lowrie (Garden City, Doubleday Anchor Books, Doubleday and Co., 1954).

[28] The Present Age, tr. by Alexander Dru, Introduction by Walter Kaufmann (New York: Harper Torchbooks, Harper and Row, 1962), p. 75.

III

A GOD FOR NATURALISM

Dewey's naturalism has been the predominant influence on at least one type of American thought. All
the essentials are there. Such thinking is pragmatic,
wordly, scientific in its methodology and totally re-
lativistic. God, as Dewey conceives Him, is in some
way the sum of the possibilities that nature exhibits.
These possibilities beckon each man and all men. They
exist already in an embryonic state, but they also
point to the possibility of a fuller and more perfect
reality as the result of action aimed at bettering the
natural situation. They are perceived by the imagination, can be clarified by the method of science, are
tested and modified by experience, and, thus reshaped
and purified, shape and purify in turn the activity
which they inspire. Dewey would rather call this the
"divine" than "God." But his meaning is clear enough.
Whatever one calls it, its present reality is no greater than that of the nature of which it is an expression.
Whatever reality it may achieve in the future will be
no greater than what nature itself achieves through a
constant evolutionary process. Where there is only nature in process, what else could be said?

One of the basic notions in Dewey's critique of
the traditional idea of God is that such a God would
lead man away from the order of nature where he has his
roots and the possibility of his human development. He
cannot see how a God who exists separately from the universe can in any way at all be a God for man. To direct man to such a God seems to dehumanize and denat-
uralize him. From one viewpoint at least, the difficulty is well taken. If, along with Aristotle, one
thinks of God as entirely separated from the world, a
pure thought of thought contemplating itself eternally,
there is reason for Dewey's criticism. Even the absolute mind of Hegel, immanent in nature as it was, Dewey thought tended to destroy the reality of the finite
and the natural. If God has any reality at all, it is
that of nature in process.

The question arises: Is it at all possible to accept Dewey's basic position and at the same time affirm the actual existence of God? It would hardly seem so. Yet an attempt has been made, and it is interesting to see what sort of a Deity emerges out of a reality in process and what can be affirmed about such a being. William H. Bernhardt, for example, a Professor of the Philosophy of Religion, has over a period of twenty-five years sought to affirm a God based on the naturalistic premises. He sees religion as a complex form of individual and group behavior which, as such, can be investigated according to the methods of the social sciences. Writing in the Iliff Review, he states:

> Three presuppositions, then, are accepted as basic to this attempt to discover the unique function of religion: first, religion must be defined in such terms as maintain a fair degree of continuity of meaning with the past; second, the data upon which conclusions are to be based consist in what has been and is acknowledged to be religious behavior; third, no special consideration is to be given to any type of religious experience.[1]

From this viewpoint he sees religion as involving three areas: religion is functional; that is, it sets up values obtainable through religious behavior; next, it provides for a reinterpretation of the world in which religious behavior takes place; and lastly, it involves techniques; that is, social and moral activities. Hence, there are areas which can be empirically investigated and about which conclusions can be drawn and religious concepts formulated.

REJECTION OF ABSOLUTE TRANSCENDENCE
It is clear that from such an approach Bernhardt can only deal with religion from a human sociological viewpoint. He sees the personalist view taken by such writers as James, Brightman, and others, as seriously lacking in any objective data. Such a justification of religion is always based on personal values which lead one to the religious option when intellectual evidence is not sufficient. To accept a God and to act religiously becomes a more personally satisfying choice than does the acceptance of a mechanistic view of the

universe. But, while this may enable one to live more
serenely in the world, it in no way provides a test for
the objective existence of God. There either is a God
or there is not, and one's personal preference has
little bearing on that fact.[2]

Nor does the more traditional view of God as an
absolutely transcendent Being Who introduces revelation
into history fare any better. In such a view there is
a discontinuity between God and man. Man is ordered to
become perfect, to achieve a pre-fall status, but finds
it impossible to do so in natural terms. If salvation
cannot come from either nature or history, then man's
only recourse is to the supernatural.

> The basic factor in the logic of absolute transcend-
> ence is the assumption that there is an absolute
> truth without which life cannot achieve its higher
> levels, and that justice demands that it be avail-
> able to us in some other way.[3]

But Bernhardt sees such a position as neither
necessary nor feasible. Such an absolute faith in an
absolutely transcendent Being is at best a substitute
for knowledge and at worst an invitation to skepticism.
It may be true that nature and man are not adequate for
the present crisis. But we have only to look at how we
have overcome our inadequacy in many areas by a piece-
meal attack on the problems facing us. Take, for example, the phenomenal progress made in medicine, psy-
chology, and the natural sciences. Why cannot we expect the same to take place in religion and morals?
Furthermore, to flee to a revealed truth is to admit
that the human intellect is inadequate to obtain any
knowledge on our natural level. But this leads logically to religious skepticism. It is better to seek
some probable verifiability than to yield to the total
inadequacy of the human intellect in this area.

He has difficulties, too, with revelation. From
a philosophical viewpoint the claims made by any type
of revelation, whether it be Judaic, Christian, or non-
Christian, must all be reduced to some sort of metanoetic knowledge. Obviously, philosophic reason is
helpless here. The acceptance of a revealed truth can

only lead to dogmatism and the recognition of the absolute claim that man's ultimate fulfillment is not of earth but can be achieved only with the help of a transcendent Absolute.

Bernhardt would rather work with what he calls the presupposition of predictive possibility.[4] This involves several factors. There is the rejection of any Absolute, as mentioned above. Secondly, there is the acceptance of a given theology as relatively true. Such a theology must have the basic capacity to relate man in value-striving and value-conserving relations with the reality we call God. Lastly, the cognitive task is one of predicting the highest possibilities which confront man, and the determination of the most efficient means of realizing these predictable possibilities.

THE GOD CATEGORY

In striving to acquire some partial knowledge of God, Bernhardt sees the fundamental problem as one of establishing a category under which the God-concept can be handled.[5] He defines a category as follows:

A category may be defined as a comprehensive class of entities, existent or subsistent, actual or ideal, real or imaginary, every member of which shares in a sufficient number of common characteristics or qualities to be classified with the others in some definite sense.[6]

Once a category is selected, it will determine the data to be considered, the hypotheses to be developed, and the methods to be used. The term "category" is not used in a Kantian sense. It is simply a methodological device looking toward clear definition and communication.

Some categories previously employed by other writers can, of course, be ruled out immediately. Such a category as Absolute Being simply will not fit an investigation which is by definition limited to the partial and the empirical. Neither will the category of Immanence-Transcendence work, since this involves a relationship of God to nature; and neither concept is

clear as yet. He further rejects the position that
God is a sensible-perceptual object. If the existence
of God can be concluded from an empirical approach, it
will be an inference, not an immediate perceptual
apprehension.

Bernhardt sees only two real possibilities for
establishing a category for Deity. The first may be
termed agathonic; that is, God as a source of value.
The second is called dynamic; that is, God as a source
of power.[7] An investigation of God as the source of
moral and personal value is generally reserved for the
mystic. It is personal rather than empirical. It will
result in predicating attributes of God which are moral
qualities, such as good, loving, father-creator, etc.
The method employed will be intuitive, metanoetic, and
even dogmatic. Bernhardt thinks one must ask what God
is before asking what values God may have for him. Now,
if the only means to obtain a God-concept are those
provided by an empirical investigation of the existential medium in which we find ourselves, then it is
clear that the category of God as source of value is
inadequate.

If we consider God, however, under the category
of Dynamic Power, then, at least, we can proceed in
accord with the demands of an empirical epistemology.
This category treats God as the source of power responsible for all process, including human life. It looks
toward a dynamism directing the processes at work in
the universe. This provides for the possibility of an
empirical method, and it will result in attributes predicated of God which are existential rather than moral-
personal.

Bernhardt sees the use of the category of Dynamism as a common sense approach which respects the inadequacy and relativism of human knowledge. It avoids
the absolutizing so characteristic of dogmatism and
follows the methodology of both natural and social
science. Since these sciences have done so much to
further our knowledge of the universe, there is every
reason to hope that the method will prove just as satisfactory when applied to God.

There are, however, two difficulties which must be faced. The first is that the category is so broad that literally every phase of the natural process will fit under it. To search for a knowledge of God under the category of Dynamic Directionality confronts the mind with every variety of motion and event and the relationships between them. But along with the difficulty there are also positive values. We are led to face reality as it is rather than to select phases of it which may be of value only subjectively. It also obviates the human temptation to orient oneself to imaginary or possible realities conceived as real in the human mode. The category of Dynamic Directionality is theocentric rather than anthropocentric. God as dynamic power is the primary role in the religious relationship. It gives the individual a truer estimate of his position in the total scheme of things.[8]

But there is a second difficulty. Bernhardt had argued against Wieman that God was in no sense at all an empirical or a perceptual object. If the empirical method is to be used, what value can it have when applied to a non-empirical reality? The solution lies in Bernhardt's definition of metaphysics as employed in an empirical methodology.

EMPIRICAL METAPHYSICS

Metaphysics may be defined as the organization of knowledge of the all-pervasive characteristics, qualities, trends or tendencies of the existential medium in order to provide a framework for the understanding of man and that in which he exists.[9]

For Bernhardt, then, metaphysics is some sort of correlation of empirical knowledge put together from the findings of the more particularized natural and social sciences. He agrees with Carnap that transempirical objects are not the proper objects of metaphysical inquiry. Furthermore, metaphysics will involve some kind of verificatory process. There is, of course, the clarification of language. This is, at least, instrumentally necessary. There are also activities or operations which are required to confirm or disconfirm the hypothesis selected for investigation. But such verification is of two kinds. There is actual or observational verification, and there is implicative or corroborative verification. It is this last type of verification which must be used by a metaphysics which investigates the existential medium with a view to discovering something about God under the selected category of dynamic directionality.

A metaphysics should also be organized around key concepts which are relevant to the age. These should be as few as possible, and Bernhardt limits them to three. They are existence, relation, and modality. Under the notion of existence will come whatever can be known about the existential medium, which is composed of things and events. Thus one will seek within the existential medium for evidence which will lead to inferential conclusions about the nature and reality of God. Bernhardt also calls this Operationalism, since meanings and interpretations are sought within the context of facts rather than in some form of Impositionism; that is, a metaphysics which asserts an Absolute Being independent of the context.[10]

Is Operationalism an adequate method for investigating the existence and nature of God? If one will reread the Symbol of Faith adopted by the Council of Trent, Feb. 4, 1546, he will find an answer to this question. The creed reads, in part, as follows:

> I believe in one God, the Father Almighty, Maker of heaven and earth, of all things visible and invisible; and in one Lord Jesus Christ, . . . by whom all things were made; . . . and again he will come with glory to judge the living and the dead.

The underlined words in the text quoted are definitely subject to operational definition and verification. "Father" means begetter, and without offspring the term is meaningless. "Maker" denotes manufacture, production and synonymous activities. And the underlined statement concerning Jesus Christ also contains terms with operational meaning and subject to operational verification. "By whom all things were made" implies creative activities, and all-inclusive activities. "And

again he will come with glory" is also subject to
operational investigation. The first two words quoted,
"I believe" are also of the same nature. Belief means
readiness to act. And the willingness or readiness to
act must eventually express itself or be denied.[11]
Bernhardt defines the word "God" as the religious name
for that in the existential medium to which men relate
themselves in search of religious values. This concept
must then be related to the metaphysical approach
sketched above.

GOD AND THE CATEGORIES OF EXISTENCE
        Existence is divided into five sub-categories;
episodicity, which indicates the nature of the existential process; directional momentum, or dynamic directionality, which seems to indicate purpose; modifiability, which concerns the external structure and internal
nature of episodes; stability, which indicates a relative constancy; and quality, which is explained as the
all-pervasive property of episodes to induce or produce
modifications in persons or other episodes.[12]

        The next question is, which of these sub-cate-
gories can be used to explicate the God-concept? Bernhardt does not think that episodicity is relevant. But
it is possible that God is a phase of many or all episodes without being identical with any of them. The
next notion, however, that of dynamic directionality,
he sees as the primary category of existence with relation to God. With regard to modifiability he would
rather substitute the capacity to modify, if one is to
predicate this of God. A relative stability seems to
be applicable to God. This stability, however, has its
negative aspect, since there seems to be that in both
nature and man which hampers the process of dynamic
directionality. Lastly, the category of quality must
apply to God since the Deity must possess the capacity
to effect and make differences. Bernhardt concludes
his discussion of the categories of existence as follows:

    In the case of God, as in that of other realities,
    we do not believe it is possible to discuss the exis-
    tence of God as such. There is no evidence to assert
    that God is a Being possessing the several properties
    or characteristics just discussed. All that we can

assert in Operational terms is that these characteristics appear. What may be required, in terms of
presuppositions, to make them possible, was considered in the articles on "The Cognitive Quest for
God" which may be considered later if time permits.
Here it is sufficient to note that Directional Momentum appears to be the primary category of Existence
in the development of Operational Theism.[13]

THE CATEGORIES OF RELATION
        These categories are based upon and in the fact
of otherness. Hence, they recognize the evidence of a
pluralistic universe. The first notion here is compre-
sence. Nothing exists in isolation. Obviously it applies to God. For God as dynamic directionality is present with all actuality. The second category of relation, emergence, does not seem to apply. It indicates,
rather, the creativity of the directional momentum.
But it would be difficult to say that God as such is
emergent. The third category is multiplicity. Can this
be attributed to God? Here Bernhardt makes a distinction.
He would rather say that God is generically one. At the
experimental level, however, directional momentum is
found varied and variable, and must be viewed as numer-
ically plural.

        The next category is selectivity or non-neutral-
ity. The terms indicate involvement and participation.
They are, therefore, the key attributes of God under
the general category of relation.

    The next relational category is <u>Selectivity or Non-
    neutrality</u>. These terms indicate involvement, en-
    gagement and participation. They also indicate
    avoidance, rejection or repulsion. This is the key
    category for the conception of God at the relational
    level. Non-neutrality or Selectivity is implied in
    the conception of Directional Momentum. It is
    Directional Momentum which is responsible for the
    changes experienced or observed within ourselves,
    within society and in the universe as a composite of
    episodes.[14]

        The last category in this series is called tran-
seunce. It is defined as the effect of the episodes

upon one another as a result of their interaction. It
indicates indirect and long range effects, the carry-
over of one episode, or at least part of an episode,
into another. In more traditional language it could be
called immortality. God is implicated in such long
range succession since it is the activity called directional momentum which makes this possible.

CATEGORIES OF MODALITY
        Modality specifies how the categories subsumed
under it function as related. The first of these sub-
sumed categories is spatiality. This does not appear
to apply to God. It could be said that God functions
within many areas. What is affirmed here is that directional momentum may transcend one episode, but transcendence of all episodes is denied. In other words, God
as directional momentum, or dynamic directionality, is
ultimately and totally immanent in every identifiable
episode. Here Bernhardt uses a somewhat unfortunate
example. He says that, if it is true the great galactic
systems emerged from some more basic field of energy,
which he previously called durationality, this would
provide an inferred context within which all that is
knowable appeared. This, he states, could very well be
an inferred "Ground-of-Being" so popular in contemporary
theology.[15] Nothing could be further from the minds of
Tillich, Heidegger, and Rahner. But neither could anyone operating under the influence of Dewey's methodology
interpret it in any other way.

        So, too, when we ask whether the next category,
temporality, will apply to God, the answer has to be
yes, in this context. If all we can know of being is
as we find it in time, then to be and to be temporal
are identical. All momentum is episodic and takes
place in time. If God is operationally verifiable within episodes and not independent of them, then God, too,
is subject to temporality. Bernhardt adds a caution
here, however. He admits he is talking about an experiential approach to God under the aspect of a religious
need. In this sense only is spatio-temporality predicated to God.

    We may summarize this attempt to base a conception of
God upon the metaphysics developed in terms of the
three undefined terms of our Limited Vocabulary.

(i). As to Existence, God is the religious name for
the Directional momentum immanent in the episodes
which together comprise the Existential Medium including man. God's activities--the retention of the
stable and the modification of existing episodes--
are discoverable within episodes at all levels.
(ii). In terms of Relation, God may be considered
compresent, engaged with and implicated in all that
occurs, the repetitive as well as the creative and/
or destructive, directly in terms of quality and indirectly in terms of generically One but operationally many. (iii). God's operations or activities
function within episodes with directionality domi-
nant over randomness. The outcomes of these activities appear in a persistent succession of culmina-
tions which are more or less temporary.[16]

OPERATIONALISM AND TRADITIONAL RELIGION
        Will Bernardt's concept of God fit in at all
with traditional theological and religious thinking?
Not without some modification, of course. He sees
Judaeo-Christianity as a result of man's attempt to
humanize an impersonal universe in terms of the father
image and the pleasure principle as explained by Freud.
This provided men with a God they could approach on human terms and provided them with a sense of security
and importance otherwise impossible in a universe in
which humankind is such an infinitesimal part.

        The same could be said of Christian Existential-
ism which tends to put man at the center of the universe
and stress human subjectivity as the only real source
of the knowledge of God. All other aspects of the existential medium are irrelevant with regard to man's religious quest. These other aspects may well be investigated by the sciences, but they have no real value
either for the understanding of man or God. It is clear
that such an attitude is directly opposed to Bernhardt's
Operationalism. From his viewpoint, a theistic view of
life would be much more pertinent, if one used it to
enable him to live more serenely and more reasonably in
a universe not made particularly for man.

        The God that emerges out of Bernhardt's investi-
gation is a power which is relative and finitely opera-

tive in the existential medium and in man. This power is immanent to that medium and in no way transcends it. While, as far as I know, he does not deny that such a power is personal, he never affirms personality of it. His view seems to be that, since personality is such a small factor in the long history of directional momentum, it is not worth predicating of God. This directional momentum operates selectively; it seems to be superior to randomness and chance; yet it is neither absolute nor omnipotent. To speak of this power in human terms is to anthropomorphize it and to commit the prideful error of likening it to man. As has been mentioned, man is at best an infinitesimal part of a universe that is by and large impersonal, inconstant, and finitely operative in space and time.

The acceptance of such a God is hardly palatable to the ordinary religious view. Such a God is not at all consistent with the God taught by traditional theism, Christian or otherwise. Much of the traditional view of God will simply have to be given up. On the other hand, Bernhardt thinks that the Operationalist view will force the individual and the group to live more realistically in a situation which has its unmanipulative factors, whether we like it or not. Man is given less chance to look to another realm for the solution to his problems, or to a father image or a personal Savior to rescue him from his sins, his guilt, and his inadequacy. The responsibility is put on man himself to make this a better world, to participate in saving himself and his society, and to accepting with religious equanimity what he cannot change.

CONCLUSION

What is interesting about Bernhardt's approach is that he is able to define an objectively "real" God starting from Dewey's non-theistic naturalism. Such a God, viewed as dynamic directionality, may be little better than the glue holding the process together; but to some extent Bernhardt does make a metaphysician out of Dewey. Those who understand metaphysics as an investigation of being will not find Bernhardt's use of the term very acceptable. They will argue that it is precisely because neither Dewey nor Bernhardt is willing to speak of being, that they condemn themselves to equate the real with the finite, the temporal, and that which is either directly or indirectly verifiable. Bernhardt himself admits that for him to be is to be temporal. From such presuppositions the conclusions are hardly surprising.

Yet it is also true that Bernhardt is willing to admit the validity of an inferential conclusion based on evidence and to admit also indirect verifiability. This can provide the possibility, at least, for an escape from Dewey's complete scientific naturalism. It does not appear to me that Bernhardt himself is able to make such an escape. He is too fond of identifying any religious or metaphysical approach which asserts an absolute as a closed system. One could just as easily argue that the naturalistic presupposition that one can think only in terms of the finite, the temporal, and the somehow-or-other-experienceable is itself an arbitrary closing off of the possibility to think in any other terms. The assertion, too, that there are and can be no absolutes comes too close to being an absolute itself to be readily acceptable. There is also in Bernhardt, as in Dewey, the tendency to regard all metaphysics as idealistic and conceptualistic systems after the manner of Descartes and Hegel.

It is true, of course, that there is little value in holding on to an absolute God, if He is merely a being created by man after his own image. But it is also true that many reputable thinkers have affirmed an absolute, omnipotent, personal God on metaphysical as well as religious reasoning. Perhaps the best that can be said of Bernhardt is that he seems to have taken St. Paul's assertion seriously; e.g., that one can know there is a God by looking at the things that are. This is more than Dewey was ever able to accomplish. In trying to conceptualize that God, however, Bernhardt is necessarily limited by a methodology whose categories are all derived from a naturalistic context.

NOTES

[1] Wm. H. Bernhardt, "Where We Are in Our Religious Thinking," in The Iliff Review, Vol. II, n.2, Spring 1945, p. 233.

[2] "The Logic of Recent Theism, Part III," in The Iliff Review, Vol. V, n.1, Winter 1948, pp. 34-35.

[3] "The Logic of Absolute Transcendence," in The Iliff Review, Vol. VII, n.1, Spring 1950, p. 35.

[4] "The Presupposition of Absolute Demand," ibid., n.2, pp. 74-80.

[5] "Religion and the Problem of Knowledge," in The Iliff Review, Vol. VIII, n.1, pp. 9-18.

[6] Ibid., p. 16.

[7] Ibid., pp. 14 ff.

[8] "The Cognitive Quest for God," in The Journal of Religion, Vol. XXIII, n.2, April 1943, pp. 91-102.

[9] "A Metaphysical Basis for Value Theory and Religion," in The Iliff Review, Vol. XV, n.2, Spring 1958, p. 14.

[10] "Operational Theism," in The Iliff Review, Vol. XVI, n.1, Winter 1959, p. 23.

[11] Ibid.

[12] Ibid., p. 24-25.

[13] Ibid., p. 25.

[14] Ibid., p. 26.

[15] Ibid., p. 27.

[16] Ibid., p. 29.

IV

GOD AND CONSCIOUSNESS

The relationship of God to human consciousness can be considered in two ways. One can take a look at the concept of God as it appears in human thought, investigating its content, questioning its origin, trying to determine its meaning. One can further ask about the value such a concept has in producing a goal for the life style and functioning of the individual. Its value, for example, may consist entirely in serving as an integrating factor for the development of the personal maturity and life view of the individual who in one way or another accepts a God. There is undoubtedly a kind of theism which stops right there. An individual may say he believes in God for the simple reason that he feels better and thinks he can live more coherently with himself and in the world than he could otherwise. It may never occur to him to ask whether or not there is any objective reality corresponding to such a concept or feeling.

The second approach is to try to find in consciousness an image or a concept of God that can be studied as an empirical fact but one which seems also to point beyond itself to some extra-mental reality. Such a concept suggests that either its origin or its goal is trans-mental and can be accepted as partial evidence for the actual existence of a Supreme Being. As we shall see, C. G. Jung, the Swiss psychotherapist, proceeds in this way. There is also a further development of this approach. Teilhard de Chardin used consciousness itself, rather than any particular concept of God, to argue that the very nature of the thinking process pointed beyond itself to a source and center of total and perfect Consciousness. We shall first consider the more empirical psychological approach and later what might be termed the cosmic approach of Teilhard de Chardin.

PSYCHIATRY AND THE GOD-CONCEPT
Am empirical science can deal only with the data

it finds on the empirical level. Physics, chemistry and biology, for example, are bound closely to the physical order by the very nature of their investigations, and any inference drawn from those investigations must be referred back to the level of experience, if they are to be verified. If this cannot be done, the inferences remain on the level of theory and hypothesis until such time as verification becomes possible. Insofar as psychiatry claims to be an empirical science, it is necessarily subject to the same rules of verification. There is, of course, a difference. Psychiatry is basically concerned with human thought processes, choices, and the whole gamut of human drives and emotions. Unless one takes a strictly behavioristic approach, this field of the human psyche is not subject to nearly as accurate measurement as is the area of the purely physical. Furthermore, while it is true that the mental and emotional activities of the human being may and do point beyond themselves to objects in the physical universe, they may also lack such reference, or may affirm realities not subject to any sort of empirical verification.

But the thought, or the choice, or the emotional drive is still a reality and may be studied as such whether or not its reference can be subjected to the area of empirical verification. It is understandable, therefore, that the empirical psychiatrist is more interested in the psychic activity itself and what it tells him about the human personality than in whatever objectivity such activity may or may not have. Hence, while God can never be the proper object of psychiatric investigation, the God-concept, as it is found in the mind of the patient, certainly can be.

It is always, of course, a temptation to speculate about the origin of such a concept or to draw conclusions about whether or not such a concept has an objective reference. To do that is properly the task of the philosopher or the theologian, not of the psychiatrist. That there have been psychiatrists who have succumbed to the temptation and who have been willing to play both the philosopher and the theologian is not unheard of. Freud's reduction of God and religion to a projection of the father-image and the need for security is well known. There are others, such as Erich Fromm in his <u>Psychoanalysis and Religion</u>,[1] who see the God-concept as having functional value for the individual, but who at the same time deny that such a concept has any transcendent reference.

THE GOD CONCEPT AS AN IDEAL

1. Fromm

In his analysis of religion and the concept of God, Fromm sides definitely with Freud and Dewey as against William James and C. G. Jung. The reasonable religion for man is always humanistic as opposed to the authoritarian modes. Self-integrity, love of one's neighbor, the striving for a better social order, are all preferable to any sort of self-abasement before a revelation or a set of rules imposed from outside. His notion of God is a faithful reproduction of Freud and Dewey. To conceive of God as a transcendent Being beyond the world is only an extrapolation of man's need for security. The God-concept is a summation of man's ideal strivings and his hopes for perfection. As such it can be productive of progress both within the individual and within society. Any other interpretation leads to a lack of proper concern for this world and makes religion consist primarily in obedience to an unseen power or power structure which is humanly humiliating. Thus:

> . . . the problem of religion is not the problem of God but the problem of man; religious formulations and religious symbols are attempts to give expression to certain kinds of human experience.[2]

In this context, the question of whether or not God exists is irrelevant. What we have here--as we have in Dewey--is a reduction of the God-concept to a pure psychic reality which has not even the possibility of a reference beyond itself. It is an abstraction of all of an individual's hopes and dreams and is purely functional insofar as it may stimulate an individual to pursue on the human level a better way of life. No one would deny that the God-concept is able to fulfill this role in the personal life of a given individual. But to arbitrarily limit such a concept to this function alone and to deny that such a concept has any other reference or value seems quite beyond the bounds of empirical psychiatry and betrays a philosophical presupposition, which can and should be arugued on the philosophical level.

2. Allport

Gordon Allport reemphasizes the positive integrating value of the God-concept for a mature personality, although he does not deny that the concept may have an objective reference. In The Individual and His Religion,[3] he states:

> A man's religion is the audacious bid he makes to bind himself to creation and the Creator. It is his ultimate attempt to enlarge and to complete his own personality by finding the supreme context in which he belongs.[4]

He finds the origins of the religious outlook in man's organic, psychological, and sociological needs. The organism, for example, is in a state of unrest, striving to fulfill its physical needs. There is always self-interested desire seeking satisfaction. And there is, of course, much juvenile interpretation of the instruction passed on by parents, teachers, and those responsible for a child's development. Yet, all of this undergoes maturation and much transformation as the human personality develops. The religious interest and the God-concept can become a master motive, consistently directive of all human activity. Thus it becomes an integrating factor, embracing all other facets of knowledge and reality. At this point, it can provide a mature view of the self and the world and what transcends both.[5]

> Religion and psychotherapy are alike in their insistence upon the need for greater unification and order in personality. Both recognize that the healthy mind requires an hierarchical organization of sentiments, ordinarily with one master-sentiment holding the dominant position.[6]

However, he is careful to draw a distinction between what psychotherapy can accomplish as contrasted with what the religious sentiment can. Psychotherapy knows the value of such an integrating motive, and it knows also the healing power of love. But it finds itself unable to do very much about it. On the other hand, Christianity, if accepted, offers a way of life based wholly on love.

In attempting to indicate more clearly the nature of the religious sentiment, Allport points out some of its main characteristics. It is, for example, well differentiated from all other motives. It is dynamic and productive of consistent conduct. It is more comprehensive than all other motives, leading to the formulation of an integrated view of life. It is, lastly and most importantly, intentional. Allport uses the term in the scholastic sense; that is, such a motive strives to attain an object, it leads toward a goal, and it is based on knowledge.[7]

When the question arises as to whether such a goal actually exists, Allport is a little more cautious. And understandably so. As has been pointed out, the data with which the empirical psychotherapist works are contained in the psychic nature of the patient. It is not precisely the function of the psychiatrist to build a philosophical argument from such data pointing to the extra-mental existence of a transcendent object. But he does not arbitrarily deny that such an object might exist. He indicates, for example, that there are those who hold that the very existence of such a dominating master motive is sufficient to validate the existence of its object. Nor does Freud's objection, that God is merely a projection of an image created by man, bother him much. What other images do we have, and in what other way could we possibly represent God? Furthermore, Anselm had argued from the concept ofGod to the actual existence of God, and the argument has survived long enough in the history of philosophy to make us cautious in rejecting it.

From his own viewpoint and on the level on which he is working, Allport sees only two possible ways of objectively validating the goal toward which the religious sentiment tends. The first is through immediate experience. This, of course, is satisfactory only to those who have had such an experience. And we have only their word for that. The second is more pragmatic. It lies in the values generated and the unity of life

attained by those who have built their mature lives on
the reality of a God corresponding however inadequately
to the religious motive which directs them. It is not
a conclusive argument, of course, but it leaves the human personality open to a reality which can be attained
in no other way.

3. Jung

C. G. Jung, the Swiss psychotherapist, emphasizes
still more strikingly the possibility of an opening of
the human personality to the transcendent. Throughout
his voluminous writings over the years, Jung always in-
sisted that he was basically an empirical psychiatrist
and neither a philosopher nor a theologian. He dis-
trusted all forms of rationalism, and was quite unwilling to have his theories regarded as anything but conclusions drawn from the experiential data he discovered
in his investigations of both the healthy and the un-
healthy personality. Jung's highly complex and involved discussion of the human psyche cannot be treated
with anything like completeness here. But some high-
lights of his approach that bear a direct relationship
to the matter under discussion in this chapter can be
pointed out without doing violence to other areas of
his thought.

THE CONSCIOUS AND THE UNCONSCIOUS

Jung sees the individual consciousness as merely
a part of a much greater whole. He likens this consciousness to an island in the ocean. This island is
small and narrow, whereas the ocean is immensely wide
and deep and "contains a life infinitely surpassing, in
kind and degrees, anything known on the island".[8] Directly below the level of personal consciousness is the
level of the personal unconscious. This consists in
what has been forgotten or suppressed and of subliminary
perceptions, thoughts, and feelings. But Jung's investigations led him to postulate the existence of a
still deeper level of the unconscious. He refers to
this as the Collective Unconscious which contains the
inheritance of the psychic experiences of the human race.
This Collective Unconscious is much more than simply
the absence of personal consciousness. It is a positive, autonomous factor capable of influencing personal
conscious activity.

This Collective Unconscious is not an arbitrary postulate. While it is true that by definition it cannot be consciously investigated, Jung found that certain symbols are so uniformly the same all over the world as to point to some sort of common capacity to form them. These symbols emerge in dreams, in magic rituals, in myths, in fairy stories, in alchemy, and in religious experiences. Hence, they seem not only to indicate a common source, but also to have a pattern of their own and to obey their own laws.

If this is true, then Jung thinks that the materialistic error--God does not exist, if He cannot be discovered behind the galactic systems--is obvious. Or, to express the same error psychologically, God can only be an illusion derived from certain motives; from the will to power or from regressed sexuality.[9] Jung does not think that by so reducing God one has escaped from Him. Any such devaluation will itself take on the position God once held and function practically in the same way. And we will pay the same service and adoration to it, as we once did to God. Man is not able to create a God, but he _is_ able to choose one.[10] Thus, one God disappears and another takes his place. Only in this sense can one speak of the death of God.

SYMBOLS OF THE DIVINE

But if God is dead only for those who cannot fit Him into a materialistic or psychological system, there is reason to suspect He may be active and creative within the larger sphere of the Unconscious. Jung devoted a great deal of time to the symbols appearing out of the Unconscious in the dreams of his patients. One of the most important of these symbols is quaternity, an age-old and presumably pre-historic symbol always connected with the idea of a world-creating deity. It is rarely, if ever, understood as such by his patients. Yet the symbol is present consistently enough for Jung to state that it is certainly a more or less direct representation of the God who is manifest in His creation.

The use of the comparative method shows without a doubt that the quaternity is a more or less direct representation of the God who is manifest in his creation. We might, therefore, conclude that the symbol spontaneously produced in the dreams of modern people means something similar--the God within. Although the majority of the person concerned do not recognize this analogy, the interpretation might nevertheless be correct. If we consider the fact that the idea of God is an 'unscientific' hypothesis, we can easily explain why people have forgotten to think along such lines. And even if they do cherish a certain belief in God they would be deterred from the idea of a God within by their religious education, which has always depreciated this idea as 'mystical.' Yet it is precisely this 'mystical' idea which is forced upon the conscious mind by dreams and visions. I myself as well as my colleagues have seen so many cases developing the same kind of symbolism that we cannot doubt its existence any longer. My observations, moreover, date back to 1914, and I waited fourteen years before alluding to them publicly.[11]

Jung is careful not to make such a symbolic representation into any sort of an argument for the existence of God. He says rightly that it proves only the existence of an archetypal God-image, which is the most that can be asserted about God psychologically. By an archetype, Jung means a content of the Collective Unconscious, a sort of counterpart to a biological instinct. These archetypes are many and universal; they are tendencies to form images in the conscious mind. These images are always symbols rather than precisely accurate, but they appear again and again in the psychic experience of the human race. Their presence, then, does warrant serious consideration. If there is a creating God, one would expect that his image would be found, however weakly and finitely, in his creation. One would further expect such an image to come to reflective awareness of itself in the only place where such awareness is possible, the conscious mind.

In his Answer to Job, Jung sees a parallel between Job's violent experience of God and our own experience today. Those experiences come to man both from within and from without, and it does little good to attempt a rationalistic interpretation. One must allow himself to be affected by the experience, however

violent it may be. It is meant to penetrate to a man's
emotional core, for only in this way can such an effect
be transformed in human knowledge. Job, for example,
experienced a baffling, contradictory God. There was
the God of love and light, and the God of wrath and
darkness, Who used Job almost as a plaything to prove
his (Job's) loyalty.

These same contradictory facets appear in the
writings of St. John. Think, for instance, of the
doctrine of total love expressed in his letters and
the dark forebodings found in the Apocalypse. Nor do
we have to look very far in our own day to experience
these different aspects of God. There is obviously
much good, much love, and much concern in the world.
But there is also evil, savagery, warfare, and hate.
In the face of this, the contemporary theist finds
himself divided in his attempt to know the God in
whom he claims to believe. The dichotomy is profound,
and the hope of reconciling the various aspects of
the God-image seems an impossible one.

Jung conceded that we are moving in a world of
images here, and that none of them touches the essence
of the Unknowable behind them.

> There is no doubt that there is something behind
> these images that transcends consciousness and
> operates in such a way that the statements do not
> vary limitlessly and chaotically, but clearly all
> relate to a few basic principles or archetypes.
> These like the psyche itself, or like matter, are
> unknowable as such. All we can do is construct
> models of them which we know to be inadequate, a
> fact which is confirmed again and again by religious
> statements.[12]

He thinks, too, that the paradoxical image as expressed
in the God-concept looks toward a resolution of the
opposites contained therein. Empirically it can be
established with a sufficient degree of probability that
there is in the Unconscious an archetype of Wholeness
which manifests itself spontaneously in dreams, and a
tendency, independent of the conscious will, to relate

other archetypes to this center. "Consequently, it does not seem improbable that the archetype of wholeness occupies as such a central position which approximates to the God-images".[13]

Jung admits that it is extremely difficult to distinguish this God-image from the Unconscious, for both are on the border line of the transcendent. But one can interpret the psychological fact as an indication of both the nearness to and the utter distance of man from God. The difficulty is further complicated by the fact that both the investigation of the God-image and the Unconscious have to be carried on within consciousness itself. But even here Jung sees a certain autonomy as characteristic of the archetype which enables one to distinguish it from the individual consciousness. Insofar as such an archetype is psychologically verifiable on the empirical level, it can also vaguely point beyond itself in obviously an inadequate way to a transcendent source which must remain ultimately unknown and unknowable.

Perhaps it should be emphasized at this point that Jung is not speaking of an innate idea of God in the Cartesian sense. He is closer in a way to what Kant meant when he spoke of the conditions that make knowledge possible. The consistent presence of a symbol for deity, however vague it may be, which Jung finds in his psychological investigation of his patients, points reasonably enough to an unconscious but common background or horizon which emerges in symbolic fashion in the patient's psychic activity. Hence the individual consciousness is thrown against the larger background of the Unconscious, which in turn is the ground of possibility for the emergence into consciousness in finite symbolism of the One Who is Consciousness in an infinite manner. Jung always insists that the God-image, in one form or another, is clearly found in psychic activity. As such it is an empirically discoverable fact. He does not argue, but merely suggests that this fact points beyond itself and gives further credibility to the theistic position. In this he quite clearly leaves the human personality open to the possibility of the transcendent in terms of both the finite Collective Unconscious and the infinitely Conscious.

PERSON, EGO, SELF

This openness of the human personality is made
still clearer, when Jung discusses the difference between the person, the ego and the self.[14] The person
is the way one presents himself in his dealings with
his peers. These dealings are at least partially directed by what people expect of one and by what one expects of himself. Such a set of manners is by no means
identical with what the individual is really like. The
ego, on the other hand, is more complete and therefore
more representative of the total personality. It is
much closer to what one really knows of himself. But
it is still empirical, and it excludes the whole area of
the unconscious. The self is still more complete than
the ego. When one speaks of "himself", for example, he
is speaking of the ego because this is what he is aware
of. The self includes the total personality, conscious
as well as unconscious elements. Now it is precisely
this totality which eludes definition or even description. One can only describe what is in his consciousness, but the unconscious must remain forever a mystery.
Hence Jung can state:

> Nobody can say where man ends. This is the beauty
> of it, you know. It is very interesting. The uncon-
> scious of man can reach--God knows where. There we
> are going to make discoveries.[15]

It is out of the unconscious, and therefore out
of the self, that the archetypes are generated. One of
these, as we have seen, is the God-image. This is also
represented as a quaternity. But it is represented, too,
as a square in a circle, or as a circle in a square.
Jung continues:

> It is an age-old symbol that goes right back to the
> pre-history of man. It is all over the earth and it
> either expresses the Deity or the self; and these
> two terms are psychologically very much related,
> which doesn't mean that I believe that God is the
> self or that the self is God. I made the statement
> that there is a psychological relation, and there is
> plenty of evidence for that.[16]

Jung further sees this symbol as a call to order
and integrity within the personality as well as an attempt

83

to reduce everything to a center. He states that it
appears in the patient's mind when there is great disorder and chaos. It is a compensatory archetype bringing with it the possibility of wholeness. It is an
invitation to the ego to locate itself in relation to
the complete self; it offers the possibility of fulfillment and understanding where before there was inadequacy
and confusion. It is, in short, a manifestation of the
constant activity of God in the world and especially in
the human psyche.

Fr. Victor White, O.P. sees Jung's position as a
challenge alike to the atheist and the theist to look
toward a more profound evaluation of what man is and
the need he has for human fulfillment.

. . . it would be grossly misleading to quote Jung
as an apologist for religion as he commonly finds it
among us Europeans today, and it is rather as a
challenge than as an apology that his work should be
viewed. Doubtless there is much in his own published
writings that has been, and will be, challenged--
both by the theologian on one side, and by the scientist and psychiatrist on the other. He himself would
have it so, and that we take nothing on faith from
him. His own challenge to the unprejudiced sceptic
and unbeliever is obvious enough. His challenge to
the professed believer is perhaps more subtle--but
no less serious. It is comparatively easy for the
man of religion to dismiss Freud, who never took religion very seriously anyhow, and whose psycho-analysis
can be labeled as 'science' and outside the concern
of ultimate beliefs and values. Jung insists that
such a dichotomy is impossible: that consciously or
unconsciously religion affects everything in our
lives. Whether we belong to any denomination or none,
he challenges us to become more conscious, more responsible, more adult in our religion--or irreligion--
if we would not destroy ourselves and our fellows.
Western man fools himself when he thinks he has outgrown religion and has no need of God--as he is learn-
ing in the bitter Nemesis to his pretensions to self-
sufficiency. But he has outgrown an infantile reli-
giousity which is no more than an escape mechanism,
an outer and theoretic compensation for inner godless-

ness in practice. When the salt has lost its savor,
it is indeed good for nothing but to be trodden down
by men.[17]

4. Teilhard de Chardin

Pierre Teilhard de Chardin also makes use of consciousness to show how man is able to point beyond himself to the transcendent. However, his perspective is
completely different from that of Jung. Jung looks toward the previous history of the race to find a common
archetype of the Deity emerging consistently from the
unconscious into human consciousness. This archetype
of the Deity, as we have seen, Jung also identified
with the notion of unity and wholeness. Teilhard de
Chardin looks rather to the future and sees the evolution of human consciousness based on a call to unity
and wholeness and to the perfection of both man and
society. In a series of essays published in this coun-
try in 1964 under the title, The Future of Man,[18] the
Jesuit scientist predicts a future state of intensified
consciousness as the term of a human evolutionary
process.

Teilhard de Chardin states there is every evidence that a vast evolutionary process has gone on over
the billions of years of history of our planet. He
thinks, too, that this process is dynamic and is still
going on today. Yet, apparently the process has come
to a halt and solidified itself, at least to the eyes
of the casual observer. Plants and animals exist in
clearly defined species, and man himself remains pretty
much the same throughout his history. But to Teilhard
de Chardin this means only that one stage of the evolutionary process has completed itself, and another is already on the way. Once matter had achieved the state of
organization and perfection necessary for the birth of
thought, for the appearance of man, that is; its task
is finished, so to speak, and the process will now continue on the human level. Furthermore, he sees this
evolution of reflective awareness and consciousness as
dramatically more dynamic and rapid than the previous
and preparatory process which took place in matter.

DIRECTIONAL EVOLUTION
If we look closely at this dynamic process in
matter toward life and consciousness, then we become

aware that this movement takes place by direction and not at random.

Research shows that from the lowest to the highest level of the organic world there is a persistent and clearly defined thrust of animal forms toward species with more sensitive and elaborate nervous systems. A growing 'innervation' and 'cephalisation' of organisms: the working of this law is visible in every living group known to us, the smallest no less than the largest.

* * * *

What can this mean except that, as shown by the development of nervous systems, there is a continual heightening, a rising tide of consciousness which visibly manifests itself on our planet in the course of the ages?[19]

Hence, the whole surge of the biological world is toward thought and man.

Indeed, within the field accessible to our experience, does not the birth of Thought stand out as a critical point through which all the striving of previous ages passes and is consummated--the critical point traversed by consciousness, when, by force of concentration, it ends by reflecting upon itself?[20]

This development of thought is most clearly evident in collective man. Basing his argument on the proposition that progress always equals growth of consciousness and this in turn manifests itself in greater and greater organization, Teilhard de Chardin argues that the growth of mankind has been unbelievable in the short time the race has spent on this planet. He points to the tremendous concentration that has taken place in the economic area as shown by the unification of the earth's energies; in the intellectual area as manifested by the unification of our knowledge in scientific systems; and, lastly, in the sociological area shown by the unification of the human mass as a thinking whole.[21] His conclusion is that the current of life has in no way come to a stop, but in emerging into thought has simply sought its essential path.

But process on this level is always self-reflec-
tive; it is aware of itself. Because of this it is
based on hope and freedom in its drive toward ever
greater unification. It is impossible to think that
this unification can come from without. This would result in mere mechanization with no further growth in
consciousness. The unanimity, if it is to take place,
must come from within. And here, too, he makes a distinction. Such a unanimity cannot be achieved only in
terms of a common body of knowledge or a common ideal.

A common body of knowledge brings together nothing
but the geometrical point of intelligences. A common aspiration, no matter how ardent, can only touch
individuals indirectly and in an impersonal way that
is depersonalizing in itself.[22]

Hence, if mankind is to continue its conscious
development, it must do so freely and by its own reflective choice not in terms of an abstract principle or a
common hope, but precisely in relation to some center
which insures complete human development. This center
must be a Being rather than a principle, for only in
this way can the individual human units involved complete themselves in truly human fashion.

This being so, the more I consider the fundamental
question of the future of the earth, the more it
appears to me that the generative principle of its
unification is finally to be sought, not in the sole
contemplation of a single Truth or in the sole desire
for a single Thing, but in the common attraction exer-
cised by a single Being. For on the one hand, if the
synthesis of the Spirit is to be brought about in its
entirety (and this is the only possible definition of
progress) it can only be done, in the last resort,
through the meeting, centre to centre, of human units,
such as can only be realised in a universal, mutual
love.[23]

Such a love is possible only if the elements involved are
all willing to center themselves, even at the expense of
themselves, on a Being available to all and present to all
This Being, of course, in the view of Teilhard de Chardin,
is the Christ of the gospels, Who as the incarnate Son of

a transcendent God, is meant to draw all things to Himself and renew all things by bringing them to their full perfection.

Furthermore, he sees in this acceptance of Christ, as the goal toward which the world and human consciousness are evolving, a solution for the age-old quarrel between the humanists and the protagonists of a transcendent, personal God. The humanists have always accused Christianity of neglecting this world and concentrating on a future one. The Christians in turn have been less than happy with what they consider an almost complete concern on the part of the humanists with only this world. For Teilhard de Chardin, the quarrel is a devisive and a weakening one. He sees no reason why one cannot combine faith in the world with faith in God. The progress of matter toward spirit and of spirit toward an ever increasing awareness of self and human destiny can reasonably terminate in Someone Who is both the beginning and the end of the process. Hence, for the humanist there is reason to look beyond matter, just as for the Christian there is reason to look into matter. The creative process itself is a sign of Divine Omnipotence, for God uses the process to achieve His ends. He also waits at the end, when the process is complete. To rise above the world, then, does not mean to despise it or reject it, but to pass through it and sublime it.

The sense of the earth opening and exploding upwards into God; and the sense of God taking root and finding nourishment downwards into earth. A personal, transcendent God and an evolving Universe no longer forming two hostile centres of attraction, but entering into hierarchic conjunction to raise the human mass on a single tide. Such is the sublime transformation which we may with justice foresee, and which in fact is beginning to have its effect upon a growing number of minds, free thinkers as well as believers: . . . .[24]

He sees also in the process, and precisely in the development of consciousness, a demand not only that all things shall not die, but that what is best of earth shall be saved. The challenge is that, either the evolutionary process must be irreversible, or that it need not go on at all. It does little good to proclaim that earth is still young and that it still has a future of billions of years; or to argue that man will one day escape from this dying planet and find means of survival elsewhere. This does no more than postpone the end.

> We cannot resolve this contradiction, between the congenital mortality of the planets and the demand for irreversibility developed by planetised life on their surface, by covering it up or deferring it; we have finally to banish the spectre of Death from our horizon.[25]

He suggests that this can be done, if one accepts the idea that at the heart of the universe there exists a divine center of convergence. He calls this the Omega point. As human consciousness increases, so will awareness of the Omega point become more widespread and can be seen more clearly as that toward which all that is real is in process. Man is, then, actually preparing himself for an escape from a dying universe. But it is not an escape that will take place outwardly into space, but spiritually and inwardly toward the heart and center of it all.

> In any event, of all the theories which we may evolve concerning the end of the Earth, it is the only one which affords a coherent prospect wherein, in the remote future, the deepest and most powerful currents of human consciousness may converge and culminate: intelligence and action, learning and religion.[26]

THE DEIFICATION OF MAN

There is, of course, a temptation here. It is the age-old temptation that man has always faced. "You shall be like Gods." As soon as we look at the tremendous progress man has made in every field since his appearance on earth, his awareness of his own special perfection can quite easily lead him to settle for himself. Why should not the future of man lie within himself? Self-reflection can easily lead to a deification of man, to a self-satisfaction that makes it possible for men to see themselves as the ultimate in a material universe over which they are constantly gaining more and more control and which they are using successfully for the betterment of man. However minute man may seem in

this universe of stars and planets, it is also true
that he is absolutely unique in terms of biological
complexity and organization. The entire universe seems
to have been in labor to arrive at the point on this
planet earth where man became a possibility and an
actuality. From this view the human species becomes
a high-point toward which all the eons of evolution
have striven. It is little wonder, then, that man
should have to face the temptation that he is himself
the Omega point.

The position is not without its adherents. Once
life has reached the reflective stage, it is thought by
some that it must now disperse itself in diverging
ethno-cultural units, and must finally culminate in
separate individualities which will represent independent, absolute summits of the universe.[27] Teilhard de
Chardin's answer is that the socialization process is
simply too evident and too strong to suppose that it is
a mere accident and will fall back upon itself and resolve itself in the individual. The process of organization toward unification is too well recognized and too
general on all other levels to favor the argument that
on the human level the individual is the ultimate.
Hence, it is hardly reasonable to conclude that there
is nothing beyond the individual man.

THE THEISTIC OPTION
Teilhard de Chardin admits that his position is
not conclusively demonstrable. The argument is open and
can be rejected at any point. Like Newman, he thinks
that its force lies in its cumulative aspect, and its
rejection will have to be for solid, positive reasons.
One can part company with the argument, but only if one
is willing to accept the alternative choice at a given
point. If one takes the third stage of the argument,
for example, that man can achieve his individual perfection only in terms of greater socialization and
solidarity with all other men, he may choose to accept
it or deny it. But either way there are consequences
that will have to be faced. To deny it means to regard
all human socialization as a mere chance arrangement.
The present universal structure of political, economic,
and social relations becomes an arbitrary system of con-
ventional and temporary expedients. Everything in the

human world is artificial in the worst sense of the word.[28]

On the other hand, if one accepts the option that individuals are ordered beyond themselves to find their fulfillment in greater and greater social unity, then he must also face other options. For the claim of Christianity is precisely that it can bring to pass man's social perfection more adequately and more completely in terms of knowledge and love than can any merely human organism. It sees itself not as some alien imposition on man, but as something brought into a human world by the man, Christ, Who asserts that in Him alone can all things come to their perfection and unification under God. This, too, is an option that must be freely chosen--and in Christian dogma it can be chosen only under grace--but it is an option one must face and also one which provides a coherent complement to the evidence already presented on the physical, biological, and social levels.

Furthermore, since it is an option, it also safeguards the individual's personal liberty even while he identifies himself with the socializing process. For socialization can be imposed on man, as it has been historically. It can also come as the result of a mechanizing and technocratic process. But to achieve it in either of these two ways can only depersonalize the individuals involved. There are those today who rightly fear what an increasingly technocratic society can do to individual liberty and initiative. But an option freely made to the socialization of man which leaves the individual and society free to further perfect itself by an ever-growing realization of what it can still accomplish in terms of knowledge and love is the greatest antidote to the fear of dehumanization. Even technocracy and the machine age can be seen as partial means contributing to the humanizing process.

Yet, it would be unreal to suppose that there are no difficulties with all this. One of the most disquieting aspects of the modern world is its growing state of dissatisfaction in religious matters. There is no present sign that religious faith is expanding.

But the fact remains that for some obscure reason
something has gone wrong between man and God <u>as in
these days He is represented to Man</u>. Man would seem
to have no clear picture of the God he longs to wor-
ship. Hence (despite certain positive indications
of re-birth, which are, however, still largely ob-
scured) the impression one gains from everything
taking place around us is of an irresistible growth
of atheism--or, more exactly, a mounting and irresistible de-Christianization.[29]

The words might well have been written last week rather
than in 1949. We are quite aware today that there is a
search going on for the more-than-human and that this
search is taking place just as much outside of organized
religion as it is within the religious structure. It is
even taking place independently of God in terms of a
purely human fulfillment. Contemporary man may not have
found himself as yet, but in many instances he has rejected the notion that God is his answer.

Teilhard de Chardin sees the difficulty as grounded in two divergent views of human fulfillment. Religion has traditionally seen man's perfection as lying
beyond the world in a God Who is totally unearthly.
Marxism, on the other hand, has preached a this-worldly
salvation for man and has always accused religion of
neglecting earth for heaven. In this respect, it is
identical with secularistic humanism, although it ad-
vocates, of course, a different method of approach.
Neither extreme is acceptable. Marxism is at best a
temporary solution. As a system it condemns evolving
man to matter at the expense of spirit. It seeks to
achieve social unity by imposing it from without and
closes man off from his higher destiny as a thinking,
loving being. But a religion that is totally other-
worldly also ignores the fact that man is born to live
in the world and to achieve his perfection in it and
through it. God Himself reached down into matter to
redeem it and sanctify it. Hence, any religion worthy
of the name has to consider the world and make it possible for spirit to continue to incarnate itself in
matter. Only in this way can religion be truly human;
and it must be, if it is to lead man beyond himself to
the divine.

CONSCIOUSNESS AND THE PERSON

Nevertheless, it must be remembered that man's progress to his own perfection and that of the species must be carried out on that level which clearly differentiates man from all others. Man appeared on this planet when matter became capable of sustaining consciousness. And for Teilhard de Chardin, consciousness and the personal go hand in hand. This is, perhaps the area where modern man faces his second great temptation, the temptation to depersonalize the world. With our admiration for science and the scientific method, we seem to be obsessed with the need to analyze everything, to break it up into intellectualized components, to reduce the universe to abstract laws and mathematical formulae. This undoubtedly leads to better understanding, but it also leads to the impersonal and the inhuman. The "I" becomes a hindrance and an impediment to scientific investigation; hence, it is eliminated. The ultimate stuff of which the universe is made and in relation to which it can be scientifically explained is called emergy. This becomes the new god, but it is a god so impersonal that it has lost its heart and its mind and no longer knows its own name.

It is here that Teilhard de Chardin would part company with someone like Bernhardt. Whatever Bernhardt untimately means by Directional Momentum as the divine element in the universe, it hardly seems to involve personality. It is true that Bernhardt never positively excludes the possibility, but he regards consciousness as too late an arrival on the scene and too minute a part of the real to give it any important place in the nature of the Directional Momentum which controls the whole process. Teilhard de Chardin would admit the point readily. But in his view it is precisely toward this appearance of consciousness, toward the birth of the capacity to know and to love that the whole evolutionary process has been striving. To discount it once it has appeared is for him the great betrayal of what it means to be man.

We have seen and admitted that evolution is an ascent toward consciousness. That is no longer contested even by the most materialistic, or at all events by the most agnostic of humanitarians. Therefore it should culminate forward in some sort of supreme consciousness. But must not that consciousness, if it is to be supreme, contain in the highest degree what is the perfection of our consciousness--the illuminating involution of the being upon itself? It would manifestly be an error to extend the curve of hominisation in the direction of a state of diffusion. It is only by Hyper-reflection--that is to say hyper-personalization-- that thought can extrapolate itself. Otherwise how could it garner our conquests which are all made in the field of what is reflected?[30]

One of the essential marks of consciousness as we experience it is to unify all things within itself, and in so doing to become ever more aware of itself. There is an ever-increasing centralizing process going on in the individual consciounesness, even while it also reaches out to associate itself with other centers of consciousness. Teilhard de Chardin is convinced that this multiplicity of limited centers of consciousness must in turn be gathered up by and sustained by an ultimate, perfect Consciousness, which, even while It binds them all together in union with Itself, must also permit them to survive as the individual centers of partial being which they are.

Seen from this point of view, the universe, without losing any of its immensity and thus without suffering any anthropomorphism, begins to take shape; henceforward to think it, undergo it and make it act, it is beyond our souls that we must look, not the other way round. In the perspective of a noogenesis, time and space become truly humanised--or rather super-humanised. Far from being mutally exclusive, the Universal and the Personal (that is to say the 'centered') grow in the same direction and culminate simultaneously in each other.

It is therefore a mistake to look for the extension of our being or of the noosphere in the Impersonal. The Future-universal could not be anything else but the Hyper-personal--at the Omega Point.[31]

Furthermore, this Center of centers, this Omega Point toward which all things converge and which sustains all, cannot just be a goal to be achieved in the future. Its

existence has to be just as real now as is that of any
of the elements, reflective or otherwise, that tend
toward that Center. Not only must such a Center be
real, but it must be present to all that it attracts
to Itself. How could it exercise such action were it
not in some way both loving and lovable at this very
moment?

> Love, I said, dies in contact with the impersonal and
> the anonymous. With equal infallibility it becomes
> impoverished with remoteness in space--and still
> more, much more, with differences in time. For love
> to be possible there must be co-existence. According-
> ly, however marvelous its foreseen future, Omega
> could never even so much as equilibrate the play of
> human attractions and repulsions if it did not act
> with equal force, that is to say, with the same stuff
> of proximity. With love, as with every other sort of
> energy, it is within the existing datum that the
> lines of force must be enclosed. Neither an ideal
> center, nor a potential center could possibly suffice.
> A present and real noosphere goes with a real and
> present center. To be supremely attractive, Omega
> must be supremely present.[32]

CONCLUSION

The purpose of these pages has not been to present a summary, even an inadequate one, of the thought
of the authors whose works have been considered. All of
them have treated many more areas than the particular
one under discussion here. But each of them has had
something pertinent to say about the God-concept, and in
some cases, about God Himself, and His relationship to
human consciousness. There are many unanswered questions
for man about the world in which he lives. Only with regard to himself and the whole question of God does he
seem to come face to face with mystery. With regard to
himself he knows his own finitude and inadequacy as an
evident fact. But he also knows his own capacity for
at least progressively infinite knowledge and ever deepen-
ing love. He knows there is a dark side to his nature as
well as a lighter side which he can make the object of
his experiential knowledge. And while it is true that
the frontiers of this darker side can be pushed back and
subjected to the light of scientific and philosophical

insight, it is also clear that it will elude his ultimate questioning and remain shrouded in mystery. For the questioner can never really include himself in the question he asks, for to do so includes the very capacity to question; and this, too, disappears in the depths not just of man but of being itself. At this point human finitude touches upon the infinite, and there is a suspicion, at least, that there is more to man than what he can submit to his empirical investigations. This very possibility of transcending the empirical self is itself the ground for a positive hope that the drive he feels to fulfill himself beyond himself is not a vain one.

Both Jung and Teilhard de Chardin make much of this human condition, when they ask the question about God. For it is persuasively reasonable that a creating God should leave a trace of Himself on the creature of His making. And one would also expect to find such a trace in that area of knowing which disappears into the infinite, whether it be the dark side of the unconscious or the lighter side of reflective reason. Certainly Jung is not surprised that, even unknowingly, man bears in his own mind and in his inherited intelligence an image of and a call from his Source. And Teilhard de Chardin reasons persuasively that there would be no reason at all for man's conscious striving, were the striving itself not reasonable or purposive. If man, and therefore consciousness, were no more than a cosmic accident, a swift passage from a void to a void, then there would be no meaning at all in pursuing the quest. The evolutionary process would come to a grinding halt, and there could be little incentive for man to continue to live with his futility. Throughout the long ages the mountains would have indeed labored to produce in this case a more tragic figure than a mouse. For an animal knows neither his own mortality nor the possibility of a future. But to produce both in man and to deny his hope for a future in the name of the knowing capacity which makes him man is to affirm that the whole process, which so purposively terminated in man, is itself without purpose. At this point the theistic option acknowledges meaning and hope and an openness to reality. Its rejection slams the door on all three.

Notes

[1] Erich Fromm, _Psychoanalysis and Religion_ (New Haven, Conn.: Yale U. Press, 1950).

[2] Op. cit., P. 13.

[3] Gordon W. Allport, _The Individual and His Religion_ (N.Y.: The Macmillan Co., 1950).

[4] Ibid., p. 142.

[5] Ibid., cf., p. 64 ff.

[6] Ibid., p. 79.

[7] Ibid., p. 124 ff.

[8] C. G. Jung, _Psychology and Religion_: West and East, tr. by R. F. C. Hull, Bollinger Series XX (Princeton, N. J.: Princeton University Press, 1969), p. 84.

[9] Ibid., p. 85.

[10] Ibid., p. 87.

[11] Ibid., p. 58.

[12] Ibid., p. 361.

[13] Ibid., p. 469.

[14] Cf. Richard I. Evans, _Conversations with Carl Jung_ (Princeton, N.J.: D. Van Nostrand Co., Inc., 1964), ch. 5.

[15] Ibid.

[16] Ibid.

[17] Victor White, O.P., _God and the Unconscious_ (London: The Harvill Press, 1952), p. 58. Cf. also the preface written by C. G. Jung and the excellent summary in an appendix by Gebhard Frei.

[18]Teilhard de Chardin, P., _The Future of Man_, tr. by
    Norman Denny, 1st American ed. (New York:
    Harper and Row Publishing Company, 1964).

[19]_Ibid._, p. 65.

[20]_Ibid._, p. 67.

[21]_Ibid._, p. 69.

[22]_Ibid._, p. 75.

[23]_Ibid._

[24]_Ibid._, p. 80.

[25]_Ibid._, p. 122.

[26]_Ibid._, p. 123

[27]_Ibid._, p. 221.

[28]_Ibid._, p. 226.

[29]_Ibid._, p. 260.

[30]Teilhard de Chardin, P., _The Phenomenon of Man_, tr.
    by Bernard Wall (London: William Collins & Co.,
    Ltd., and New York: Harper & Brothers, 1959),
    p. 258.

[31]_Ibid._, pp. 259-260.

[32]_Ibid._, p. 269.

V

THE GOD OF FAITH

An acceptance of God which is based on, or at least includes, some sort of faith is common enough in the history of theism. By faith here is meant an acceptance of a truth which the human intellect cannot fully comprehend, yet one to which it freely assents because of one motive or another. The truth in question is not unreasonable. It is, however, neither logically compelling nor experientially evident. There may be advantages both in accepting it and in rejecting it. The intellect remains rooted in between the two poles, and, if left to itself, will never reach a decisive conclusion. There is the need in such a situation for the entrance of another factor, human or divine, to tip the balance, as it were; to incline the human intellect one way rather than another. It is here that the element of human freedom emerges, that the will chooses to settle for this option rather than that. The theistic option: there is a God, is the result, then, of an interplay of both intellect and will which leads the individual to a conclusion which he could never reach on the level of pure intellectual consideration or on that of experiential evidence.

While every act of faith is concerned with a truth which may be expressed in propositional form, theologians will differ with each other on the importance of such propositional expression. The difference is more one of emphasis than of essence. Always there is another person involved because of whose trustworthiness or authority the believer assents. This may be a parent, a teacher, a loved one, or, in the case of divine faith, God Himself. One could say, for example: I believe in you; therefore, I believe in what you have said. Or" I believe what has been asserted because I believe in you. In either case there is a personal element and an impersonal expression of what the person involved has said, or promised or revealed. Most of the authors to be considered in this chapter tend to put the emphasis on the person to be believed rather

than on an impersonal statement of what is to be believed. Thus, the theistic option is primarily an
assent to the reality of a living person, in this case,
God. It includes, then, an encounter with such a person, an experiential contact--however that may be ex-
plained--rather than an impersonal exposure to credal
propositions. However necessary a part of faith these
might be, they are not the primary object of the believing act. In such an approach, "Thou art my God,"
becomes much more essential than, "There is a God."

A TRADITIONAL VIEW
       In order to understand this personal approach
better, let us first look at a traditional approach and
one more common historically, at least in some theological circles. This position is basically that of St.
Thomas Aquinas.[1] Aquinas was convinced that the existence of God could be philosophically demonstrated.
One, therefore, who has been through the demonstrative
process and who understands its logical necessity is
intellectually compelled to accept the conclusion: God
exists. There is no question of faith here. Faith
enters the picture only later, when one is confronted
with truths revealed by God, which truths are beyond
the range and capability of the human reason to comprehend. The individual will accept such revealed truth
only because of the authority of the God revealing them
and then only because he is aided interiorly by divine
grace to do so. Such truths, moreover, always remain
in the realm of mystery and, as such, are never fully
comprehensible to human reason. It is a classic position, and it has the advantage of firmly grounding the
existence of God on reason before the reason is presented with revealed mystery and truths supra-rational
in their content.

       Aquinas does admit, however, that there are
truths, which natural reason can theoretically achieve,
but which as a matter of fact are achieved by most men
only through faith. He includes among these the existence of God, the immortality of the human soul, and
the fact that God is one. He sees this as only reasonable. For, while such truths can be philosophically
established, the demonstrative process is necessarily
a long and arduous one. It involves much prior know-

ledge, none of which is easy, and it also involves a thorough training in metaphysics, not exactly the most popular of human approaches to an understanding of the way things are. Most people, concerned as they are with making a living and caring for a family, simply do not have the time to go through so long a process. Others, who may have the time, are by disposition not inclined to spend that time in this way. And still others do not have the ability to pursue the necessary studies, even if they wanted to. For all such, then, it is better and more reasonable to accept even the existence of God on faith.

Despite all that has been written on the topic, I do not think it is completely clear whether such an act of faith in the existence of God is natural or supernatural; that is, whether it is based on natural though inadequate human reasoning or human testimony, or whether it also requires divine grace. It seems to be true, however, that even those who are convinced that the existence of God can be conclusively demonstrated began by believing in God before they went through the demonstrative process. Hence, it becomes psychologically impossible to determine where faith leaves off and reason begins; or, indeed, if reason ever manages to free itself from faith in the process. This is, perhaps, one reason why authors like Gabriel Marcel[2] insist that the proofs for God's existence are little more than logical explications of a truth already accepted through faith.

But most authors in the thomistic tradition maintain a clear distinction, theoretical at least, between the fact of God's existence and the acceptance of supernatural truth revealed by God. Even C. Cirne-Lima[3] who places much more emphasis on faith in the Person revealing than on what is revealed keeps to the traditional distinction between the existence of God and His revealed truth. But the position we are primarily concerned with here sees theism in its totality as a free option. There is in general an agreement among those who hold the position that the existence of God cannot be philosophically demonstrated. Hence, one must either approach God in faith or not at all. On the other hand, the God-option is not irrational. Reason can and does suggest the reality of God, even though it cannot demonstrate his existence.

THE SAFER WAY

To look upon theism as the safer of two options was given dramatic presentation by Blaise Pascal in the 17th century.[4] He proposed the option as one alternative in a wager. When the existence of God cannot be known for certain, one is forced to wager either that God exists or that He does not. By the mere fact of birth everyone is in the game, whether he likes it or not. And his whole future is colored and even determined by how he makes his wager. To this wager the individual brings his reason, an understanding of what he may gain or lose, and the knowledge that one day he will be declared a winner or a loser. If he chooses to bet that God does not exist, he frees himself from certain laws and obligations here on earth, but he is, of course risking eternity. If, on the other hand, he bets on God's existence, he assumes certain obligations involving a whole way of life, but he also assures himself of a successful eternity. What the theist wagers and throws into the balance is of small significance compared to what he can win. But the atheist is willing to wager his eternal salvation against what the theist considers of little value.

For Pascal the only reasonable alternative is to wager that God exists. If there is a God, then one wins everything. If there is not, then he literally loses nothing. Just the opposite is true of the atheist. If he wins his bet, he will not even be around to collect. In this case, winning is equivalent to losing. If, however, he loses, then he loses an infinite and eternal reward. The only logical conclusion, then, is to wager that there is a God. The risk is minimal compared to what the atheist risks. In fairness to Pascal, it should be pointed out that his theistic position is not based entirely on this sort of gamble. He uses it only as one possible approach to the acceptance of God. Yet it is an approach that has been fascinating enough to win a place in the human inquiry about the reality of God.

The inadequacies are obvious enough. Where, for

example, does one stop choosing the safer option? If one chooses to bet that there is a God, how does one go about living out this option? According to which religion is it safer to serve God? Does one throw in one's lot with any religious leader who may come along, simply because it may be safer to do so? And so on. The suspicion arises that the man who took the wager seriously might very well lose his mind in his constant effort to choose safer and ever safer options. But the wager does have its appeal for right-minded people who do not view the existence of God as susceptible of intellectual demonstration. The willingness to believe that there is a God is certainly more prevalent than is the willingness to reject Him. And, as Pascal points out, the alternatives do have drastic consequences. The dice in this case are loaded in favor of the theistic position. But, then, if there is a God, they would be. In this sense, the theistic option seems to justify itself.

THEISM AS A LIVE OPTION

William James in his essay, "The Will to Believe,"[5] is sympathetic to Pascal's position, although he finds it inadequate. James would rather speak of options which are both alive and forced. By a live option he means one which is of interest to us. A forced option is one which presents us with alternatives, one of which we must choose whether we like it or not. Such options always involve uncertainties and can never be submitted to the scientist's demand for compelling evidence. Nevertheless, we all face such situations where we must humanly make a choice, and where the refusal to choose is itself a choice.

. . . are there not somewhere forced options in our speculative questions, and can we (as men who may be interested at least as much in positively gaining truth as in merely escaping dupery) always wait with impunity till the coercive evidence shall have arrived? It seems a priori improbable that the truth should be as nicely adjusted to our needs as that.[6]

Moral questions, for example, are of this type; for pure intellect alone or scientific investigation by itself can never determine the moral value of a given

kind of activity. "Science says things are: morality
says some things are better than other things."[7] Yet
no man can avoid the choice of accepting a moral
stance toward the world, himself, and his fellow man.
To remain amoral is itself a moral choice. As James
sees it, the religious hypothesis is also a live and
forced option. In fact, it is a momentous option.

We are supposed to gain, even now, by our belief,
and to lose by our non-belief, a certain vital good.
Secondly, religion is a _forced_ option, so far as
that good goes. We cannot escape the issue by remaining sceptical and waiting for more light, because, while we do avoid error in that way, _if reli-
gion_ _be_ _untrue_, we lose the good, _if_ _it_ _be_ _true_,
just as certainly as if we positively chose to dis-
believe.[8]

The skeptic, then, does not really avoid the option. Rather, he opts for a certain particular kind of
risk. He chooses to risk the loss of truth rather than
to take a chance on error. He is backing the field
against the religious hypothesis, just as the believer
is backing the religious hypothesis against the field.
This is not a case of intellect against all passions,
but only intellect with one passion laying down its law.
"Dupery for dupery, what proof is there that dupery
through hope is so much worse than dupery through fear?"[9]
What James is really arguing for is the right of the
individual to believe in God and religion, even if the
evidence is not compelling, in the face of the scientific demand that only adequate evidence (as defined by
the scientist) be grounds for belief. For the religious claim may be valid, and no one can tell me that I
must forfeit my chance to be on the winning side simply
because he may consider the evidence to be insufficient.

I confess I do not see how this logic can be escaped. . . . When I look at the religious question as it really puts itself to concrete man, and
when I think of all the possibilities which both
practically and theoretically it involves, then
this command that we shall put a stopper on our
hearts, instincts, and courage, and _wait_--acting of
course meanwhile more or less as if religion were _not_

true--till doomsday, or till such time as our intellect and senses working together may have raked in
evidence enough,--this command, I say, seems to me
the queerest idol ever manufactured in the philosophic cave.[10]

Not only does man's nature lead him to accept
the theistic option as the meaningful one, but he also
finds the consequences of such a choice pragmatically
beneficial. James thinks that man has a real need of
God and that the acceptance of a God helps him to get
the most out of the game of existence. To hold a God
distinct from the universe and on Whom the universe
depends promises more for the future than does the
blind force of the materialists. If we look only to
the past, it is true that it is almost impossible to
choose between theism and atheism. The world is what
it is and will continue to be so, whether God or matter
is its ultimate principle. But when we look to the
future, a decided difference begins to manifest itself.

For what can materialism promise? From this
viewpoint the world is doomed, and materialism can
speak only of tragedy and extinction. The world cannot
survive, nor can man. All will disappear leaving
neither a trace nor a memory. The theistic option offers just the opposite. It guarantees an ideal order
that shall be permanently preserved. The theist can
look for the triumph of good over evil. He lives with
the hope of immortality. He believes in a providence
that directs all things to their fulfillment. He knows
why he finds nature and himself inadequate, and he looks
forward to a remedy for this in God. Even if this
world passes, God remains mindful of all the old ideals
and will bring them elsewhere to perfection. Materialism is a denial of eternity and of hope. Theism affirms
an eternal moral order and frees us to hope in the
future. From a purely pragmatic viewpoint, theism is a
reputable position. It works better, and, according to
James, this itself is a warrant for its truth.

It does not seem that James has added very much
to Pascal's wager. Nor would most theists find it any
more attractive. Very few of those who believe in God
would put their faith on the level of a reasonable

gamble. And, even if some did, the gamble gives absolutely no assurance that God really exists. Betting
that heads will turn up rather than tails when a coin
is flipped still does not give me any knowledge at all
that it will be heads. Even hoping it will be heads
because I wagered that way will not make heads come up.
This is where the "will to believe" becomes the wish it
were so. James had undoubtedly provided a service in
insisting that one has the right to be a theist, even
if others do not consider the evidence for God's **exis-**
tence sufficient. But he pushes the argument too far.

This becomes especially apparent when he attempts
to further substantiate his belief in God by pointing
out its pragmatically beneficial results. One could
very easily be led to accept almost any position simply because of the personal good which might be involved. Hence, one's belief could change from one
month to another, from one situation to another. In
this regard, J. Hick's criticism is certainly to the
point.

But when we have spelled out James' conception of
faith thus far, we cannot help asking whether it is
much better--or indeed any better--than an impressive recommendation of "wishful thinking." Is he
not saying that since the truth is unknown to us we
may believe what we like and that while we are about
it we had better believe what we like most? This is
certainly unjust to James' intention; but is it unjust to the logic of the argument? I do not see
that it is: and I therefore regard James' theory as
open to refutation by a reductio ad absurdum.[11]

FAITH AS A WORLD VIEW
There is another view which places the acceptance of God's existence entirely within the realms of
faith itself, at least the acceptance of the God of
Christianity Who revealed Himself and sent His Son to
lead man to salvation. Luther had said that God and
faith belonged together; so much so that statements
about God made from any other point of view were not
statements about God at all. The approach became quite
popular, particularly in Germany in the 19th century.
It was primarily an answer to Kant's critique and his
limitation of human reason to the world of sense phe-

nomena. If faith could be put into a realm all its own and the existence of God included in faith, then it was obvious that Kant's criticism of reason's ability to prove the existence of God would have no effect on the believer at all. Kant's negative influence on the capacity of human reason is still evident in the position as it is held today. But its adherents have had to keep a wary eye also on the linguistic and analytic philosophers who attack all unverifiable propositions as nonsense. As a result an attempt is being made at present to develop a logic peculiar to faith and to indicate how such propositions which express the truths of faith might possibly be called verifiable.

In his book, The Meaning of Revelation,[12] H. Richard Niebuhr begins by accepting a fundamental historical relativism without, however, conceding that this necessarily leads to skepticism. The Christian revelation, like any other historical event, is just as much subject to such relativism. It occurred in time and in a given culture. This revelation comes down to us mediated by various epochs and a variety of cultures. There is simply no way to avoid this or to deny that it has been subject to and conditioned by these cultures. In other words, Christianity has a history, and like any historical event it is subject to interpretation, to selection, and to criticism. It is this critical factor which keeps Christianity from being completely subjective and which enables it to affirm by faith the independent reality of what is mediated through sense and to discriminate between uninterpreted and unintelligible impressions and constant, intelligible content.

> If we are confined by our situation to the knowledge of God which is possible to those who live in Christian history we are not thereby confined to a knowledge of Christian history but in faith can think with Christianity about God, and in Christianity have experience of the being who is the beginning and the end of this historic faith.[13]

Theology can operate reasonably only within such a history. For it is only within the limited point of view of Christian faith that a reality discloses itself which invites all the trust and devotion of finite, temporal man.

Such a theology of revelation is objectively rela-
tivistic, proceeding with confidence in the independent reality of what is seen, though recognizing
that its assertions about that reality are meaningful only to those who look upon it from the same
viewpoint.[14]

This standpoint includes not just intellectual propositions about the God Who reveals Himself but value judgments as well, judgments which involve the religious
response of the whole feeling, willing, desiring person.

When a Christian says 'God,' he does not mean that a
being exists who is the beginning of the solar system or of the cosmos, or the great mathematician who
figured out a world in which mathematicians can take
delight. What he means, what he points to with the
word 'God,' is a being infinitely attractive, which
by its very nature calls forth devotion, joy and
trust. This God is always 'My God,' 'Our Good,'
'Our beginning,' and 'Our end,'[15]

Hence, it is not enough just to look at revelation from an extrinsic historical viewpoint; but it is
necessary to view it from within. All knowledge of God
is acquired only in terms of a lived faith, a developing inner experience which results from being a member
of a community which shares such a faith and which as a
result acquires deeper and deeper insight into the God
Who reveals Himself to this community.

This is the sum of the matter: Christian theology
must begin today with revelation because it knows
that men cannot think about God save as historic,
communal beings and save as believers. It must ask
what revelation means for Christians, rather than
what it ought to mean for all men, everywhere and at
all times. And it can pursue its enquiry only by
recalling the story of Christian life and by analyz-
ing what Christians see from their limited point of
view in history and faith.[16]

Nevertheless, revelation reaches out beyond its
limited sphere and illuminates all the rest of our own
personal history and the history of the world. It is

the intelligible event which makes all other events
intelligible. It helps us see the world as having purpose, order, and meaning. It casts the light of theism
over everything and sees Christ and God as giving direc-
tions not only to the world but also to our own involvement in it. It is as much part of the heart as it is
of the head, and it brings into harmony these basic
elements in our nature. For the heart not only understands what it remembers of the past, but it is also
driven to remember what it had forgotten. It enables
us, too, to focus more clearly on the present and to
understand something of what is happening, at least to
the extent that we can see it as the present course of
God's redeeming process.

> Not with complete clarity, to be sure, yet in a
> glass darkly, we can discern in the contemporary
> confusion of our lives the evidence of a pattern in
> which, by great travail of men and God, a work of
> redemption goes on which is like the work of Christ.
> We learn to know what we are doing and what is be-
> ing done to us--how by an infinite suffering of the
> eternal victim we are condemned and forgiven at the
> same time; how an infinite loyalty refuses to aban-
> don us either to evil or to nothingness, but works
> at our salvation with a tenacity we are tempted to
> deplore. The story of Jesus, and particularly of
> his passion, is the great illustration that enables
> us to say, 'What we are now doing and suffering is
> like this.'[17]

Revelation is in a sense its own validation, for
it does give meaning and fruitfulness to the lives of
those who accept it. Yet Niebuhr is not willing to
settle for the truth of revelation merely on subsequent
pragmatically beneficial effects. It possesses a prior
validity and an intrinsic truth in which all of its
effects are grounded. But what is it we are certain of
as we regard the illuminating point in our history and
how do we become certain of it?[18] To answer the question, Niebuhr begins by distinguishing between knowledge of things and knowledge of persons. In our knowledge of things we are the only active being. The object which is known is passive. It is manipulated by
us for our own ends and purposes. We ask the questions,

judge the answers, try to discover what is hidden. This sort of knowledge is also impersonal. The knower must maintain a distance and a disinterest in his personal concerns in order to come to an objective grasp of the object in itself.

But the situation is quite different when we come to a knowledge of other persons. Here a certain reciprocity of communication is required. To know another person we must begin with the activity of that other, just as the other must begin with our activity, if he is to know us. Unless the other person reveals himself to us, we shall never know him. Neither will anyone else know us, unless we are freely content to reveal ourselves to him. Selves are known in their actions, or they are not known at all. Hence, there is free choice here on both sides. There is a choosing and a being chosen. There is an opening of oneself to another and vice-versa. And neither self is ever the same once the process has begun. Impersonality gives way to personality, and immediately the knowledge involved goes far beyond any abstract or merely scientific knowledge.

With regard to revelation, then, what person is it who reveals himself in our history in such fashion that we gain a certainty which forces us to seek an intelligible unity in all our life as selves? Neibuhr does not think it is basic enough to say the person is Christ.

When we say revelation we point to something in the historical event more fundamental and more certain than Jesus or than self. Revelation means God, God who discloses himself to us through our history as our knower, our author, our judge and our only savior. 'All revelation,' Professor Herman writes, 'is the self-revelation of God. We can call any sort of communication revelation only then if we have found God in it. But we find and have God only when he so incontestably touches and seizes us that we wholly yield ourselves to him. . . . God reveals himself in that he forces us to trust him wholly.'[19]

Now to enter into such a moment means to encounter a person. We no longer simply acknowledge
that there is a God, but we say with our whole person,
"Thou art my God!" There is no impersonal proposition
enunciated here about the nature of things, but an act
of faith, of confidence, and commitment. When we fail
in faith from now on, we fail in this faith. When we
sin, we sin against this person. God is now our contemporary God, revealing Himself in every event to our
lives. Niebuhr is willing to recognize the difficulties in such an explanation of revelation. Does it not
become so mystic an event that it is no longer able to
be discussed in ordinary language? Furthermore, traditional Catholicism has always spoken of revelation as a
given supernatural knowledge of our last end and the
means to attain it. Protestantism, too, has spoken of
revelation as being contained in the Scriptures, which
present the truths by which we are to be saved. There
are futher difficulties. If all our knowledge of God
and His saving truth comes from a personal encounter
with Him, what does one do with a knowledge of the
moral law, which certainly seems to antedate a revelation and is even recognized by those who claim no revelation? Is there not also some pre-knowledge of God?
Otherwise how would we recognize the God Who reveals
Himself?

Niebuhr does not deny the validity of any of the
objections proposed. His solution consists, rather, in
an attempt to incorporate them and harmonize them by a
series of distinctions between impersonal and personal
knowledge, between knowledge acquired naturally and
knowledge given in revelation. It could hardly happen,
for example, that the knowledge of God derived from the
revealing moment be so mystic as to be incommunicable.
There is no question here of a revelation of the inti-
mate nature of God as He is in Himself. And the truth
which the individual apprehends is grasped only darkly,
and it is shared by the other members of the community
of faith. Further, revelation does not absolve either
the individual or the community from the obligation of
a continual inquiry into the profundity of the revealed
truth. There is no insurmountable difficulty either in
formulating such insights as are had from revelation
into propositions. But it must always be remembered

that there is a world of difference between the attitude of one looking at those propositions from the outside, as it were, and one who has received the truth in faith and who has committed himself to a living out of its implications.

With regard to the teachings of the moral law, Neibuhr agrees with Kant and others that there is in the mind and heart of man at least a rudimentary awareness of morality, and that this is there even before man may have come to a knowledge of God. But, again, there is a vast difference between morality seen as a sort of natural instinct and the morality one meets with in the revealing moment. There is a definite change which takes place which marks a revealed morality as the disclosure of God as a person. In the first place, there is a definite intensity of imperativeness that accompanies God's revelation of Himself as a person. At this point the moral law no longer states what we must demand of ourselves, nor what the best reasoning of the best men demands. Neither can it be equated with the demands made by the society in which we live. All such demands are escapable. Through the revelation of God the moral law is known as the demand of One from Whom there is no flight, Who respects no persons, and makes no exceptions. Transgressions of the law no longer appear as acts which go against our nature, or our social or biological life. They may well do this. But now they are seen for what they really are: violations of the whole orderly plan of the universe and a striking out against God Himself.

They do not merely violate the soul and body of the self or its community; they do violence to the body of God; it is his son who is slain by our iniquity. There is no escape from the judgment of that transgression or from the necessity of making good that violation through any hope of forgetfulness on his part or through a death which would remove us from his sphere. The imperative behind the law is the imperative of the faithful, earnest, never-resting, eternal self. As the prophets did not declare to Israel a new morality but directed attention to the eternal imperative behind a nomadic morality, so Jesus Christ gives us, first of all, no new ethics but reveals the lawgiver whose implacable will for the completion and redemption of his creation does not allow even his most well-beloved son to exempt himself from the suffering necessary to that end. The righteousness of God which is revealed in Jesus Christ is the eternal earnestness of a personal God.[20]

The second change which is effected in the moral law by revelation is that it becomes ever more extensive and intensive in its application. No longer is the law seen as peculiar to a given society, or applicable only to those who are good. The moral law is grasped as absolutely universal. Now there is neither Jew nor Greek, Gentile nor Christian, but all the others whose rights and dignities demand our virtuous repect. He sees here, too, that the law becomes a personal accusation of the shortcomings and sins of the individual. Just as revelation informs us that it is we who must keep the law, so it confronts us with the guilty knowledge that we have not always kept it in the past. The reciprocity of personal obligation is emphasized in a new way between person and person and between us and a revealing God. There is more yet. Revelation enables us to see further that the law is not just an obligation but a call to love as fully as possible both the God Who gives the law and the persons who come under it. The law, then, points beyond itself to a potentiality which must be fulfilled by our own work and willingness to bring the law to its perfection and fulfillment under God. "To be a man does not now mean to be a lord of the beasts but a child of God."[21]

Some sort of the same revolutionary change takes place in our knowledge of the God of revelation, when we compare it to the dim pre-knowledge of God which is natural to all men. Niebuhr recognizes that there is some basic primitive religion found throughout the history of man. We find in all men a radical awareness of dependence and incompleteness. We all look forward to the ultimate preservation of the values we cherish most. We seek a guarantee for the existence which we cannot give. We suspect, at least, that there has to be some final ground for the realization of the ideals of truth, beauty, and goodness which we prize so highly. Plato and Aristotle did speak of the Form of the Good and the Unmoved Mover. All this is as it should be.

But when God discloses Himself to us in the moment of revelation, an entirely new orientation takes place in our knowledge. This is a knowledge of God as a person, not knowledge about God. This is the meeting with One Whom Jesus Christ called "Father". The philosopher may have known that God is One, but revelation presents us with an entirely different idea of His unity. He presents Himself to us not as the One beyond the many, but as the One Who acts in and through all things. He is not the unconditioned, but the conditioner.[22] He is not Jupiter, the king of the lesser gods, but the enemy of these. He is no longer a perfection of our own partial unity, but rather an illuminator of our own lack of unity and order. The unity toward which He orders us is different from what we expected. For Him our last things are first and our first things last. The same is true when we consider His power and His goodness. In all these areas revelation demands a re-thinking of all our previous notions of what God must be like.

> He fulfills our expectation of the intrinsic good and yet this adorable goodness differs from everything we had expected, and puts our expectations to shame. We sought a good to love and were found by a good that loved us. And therewith all our religious ambitions are brought low, all our desires to be ministers of God are humbled; he is our minister. By that revelation we are convicted of having corrupted our religious life through our unquenchable desire to keep ourselves with our love of our good in the center of the picture. Here is goodness that empties itself, and makes itself of no reputation, a goodness that is all outgoing, reserves nothing for itself, yet having all things. So we must begin to re-think all our definitions of deity and convert all our worship and our prayers. Revelation is not the development and not the elimination of our natural religion; it is the revolution of the religious life.[23]

Only the believer, then, can really talk about God and only the one who approaches Him in faith can understand, however darkly for the present, the world, himself, and human history. Yet the knowledge that

faith brings is essentially no different intrinsically
from that which can be achieved on the purely human
level. The function of faith seems to consist in a
re-orientation of the subject to a personal relationship with God and a commitment to a life lived in terms
of this relationship. Faith gives a new perspective
rather than a new truth. He would agree with Aquinas
that human reasoning is often mixed with error and is
frequently led astray by imagination. Many retain
their doubts even in the face of objectively demonstrated conclusions. Faith in such instances can and
does act as a bulwark against those who lead human beings astray and cause them by apparently sound arguments to take a view of the world which is radically a
false one.[24]

On the other hand, Niebuhr would not agree that
faith is fundamentally the acceptance of a kind of
truth which is impervious to natural human reason. The
relationship which faith is meant to establish is always a highly personal one between the individual and
his God. In fact, he sees both Protestantism and Roman
Catholicism as posing obstacles to such a relationship.
Protestantism tends to substitute faith itself for God,
and Catholicism, of course, interposes an institution
between the individual and God. But for the man who
can believe, who can open himself to a personal God, the
true meaning of history and God's presence in it will
be made manifest. God Himself will come to him and
make His reality a truth beyond all doubt.

AN EPISTEMOLOGY OF FAITH
Professor John Hick of Cambridge University holds
a similar position,[25] but he is more concerned about
its philosophical and epistemological implications. He
understands faith as a way of interpreting the world
and our experience of it. Hence, faith is a knowledge;
and, while its object may be unique, its basic epistemology is the same as that of all knowing. The world
is essentially significant. We live in it, understand
it, at least partially, and are able to cope with it.
Our environment is radically intelligible. "Significance, then, is the most general characteristic of our
experience."[26]

The subjective counterpart to such significance is interpretation. This suggests the possibility of differing judgments. It involves the possibility of differing accounts of the same subject matter. Interpretation includes, too, different levels of significance. Confronted with one and the same object one person identifies it as a thing, another as a book, and still another as a treatise on chemistry written in German. One type of significance, then, may be imposed upon and interpenetrate another. Furthermore, significance is pointed toward action. ". . . . it is only when we have begun to act upon our interpretations, and have thereby verified that our environment is capable of being successfully inhabited in terms of them, that they become fully real modes of experience."[27]

The situations in which interpretative significance occurs are also multi-leveled and penetrate each other. We live, for example, in the physical world of nature with which we have to deal and whose laws we must learn, if we are to survive. We take that world for granted, but there is a basic interpretation here that such a world is really there, that it is varied and multiple, and that it is not just a projection of our mind. We judge, too, that this natural environment is inhabited by others like ourselves; and, immediately, there is imposed upon the natural world of nature another insight that we are related to these others in a different way. There arises a recognition of the need for cooperation, of responsibility and respect, a judgment of how we ought to act in relation to these others. The whole foundation is there for an ethical significance which presupposes the natural and penetrates it through and through. This is also an interpretative judgment, but it is a far more voluntary one than the judgment that we are involved in a material universe. It is easier to choose not to act responsibly than it is to choose to think there is no such thing as matter.

Hick then proceeds to push the point further. "As ethical significance interpenetrates natural significance, so religious significance interpenetrates both ethical and natural."[28] Thus the divine can be seen as the highest order of significance, mediating neither of the others and yet being mediated through them. The difference here is that for the believer the religious significance of life is a total interpretation of what all that is is really like.

> The monotheist's faith—apprehension of God as the unseen Person dealing with him in and through his experience of the world is from the point of view of epistemology an interpretation of this kind, an interpretation of the world as a whole as mediating a divine presence and purpose. He sees in his situation as a human being a significance to which the appropriate response is a religious trust and confidence. His interpretative leap carries him into a world which exists through the will of a holy, righteous, and loving Being who is the creator and sustainer of all that is. Behind the world—to use an almost inevitable spatial metaphor—there is apprehended to be an omnipotent, personal Will whose purpose toward mankind guarantees men's highest good and blessedness. The believer finds that he is at all times in the presence of this holy Will. Again and again he realizes, either at the time or in retrospect, that in his dealings with the circumstances of his own life he is also having to do with a transcendent Creator who is the determiner of his destiny and the source of all good.

> Thus the primary religious perception, or basic act of religious interpretation, is not to be described as either a reasoned conclusion or an unreasoned hunch that there is a God. It is, putatively, an apprehension of the divine presence within the believer's human experience. It is not an inference to a general truth, but a 'divine-human encounter,' a mediated meeting with the living God.[29]

The religious interpretation of the universe is just that. It is a judgment which always leaves something unresolved in its wake. The facts could be interpreted otherwise, as they have been and are still. The realist cannot prove to the idealist that our senses make contact with the physical world. He interprets the data of experience in this way. So, too, with the awareness of moral obligation. The ethical man accepts the responsibility of living under social obligations.

And once he comes to terms with his interpretation, he
neither requires nor can he conceive of any further
validation for his position. The same is true of the
apprehension of God. The theist finds himself interpreting his experience in this way. He lives with the
assurance of a God-directed universe, although he is
unable to prove by any dialectical process that God
exists.

The next question that arises is: Why, if there
is a God, should He make Himself known in such an indirect manner? The answer lies in a respect for man's
personal freedom and responsibility. As we have seen,
the theistic attitude is attained as a voluntary interpretation of the world and man. Now, where options are
concerned, freedom is involved. And this freedom is involved most perfectly in the case of the God-option.
This becomes clear, when we compare our cognition of the
divine with that of the physical world and that of the
moral order. There is very little freedom involved in
accepting the world with which our senses bring us into
contact. Matter exerts its pressures on us, whether we
like it or not. There is more freedom with relation to
the moral order, but even here most men feel the urge
of moral obligation. We may reject such an obligation
in specific instances, but conscience is never wholly
quiet. The act of deliberately silencing it is more
inhuman than not. In other words, we are free to
choose against conscience; but, when we do so, it is
generally in terms of a free refusal to let the real
situation manifest itself to us. We elect to allow
selfishness and egoism to triumph over the validity of
the moral claims upon us.

When we approach the God question, Hick sees
our cognitive freedom at its maximum. For on this
level we are concerned primarily with an I--Thou relationship. Man is a person who comes into confrontation with another Person. Now a person is always as
such an inviolable center of consciousness. It can
only be known by others, if it freely opens itself,
communicates itself to them. At any point one can refuse such openness and such communication. The difficulty is increased, when we consider the problem from
the side of God. In the first place, God is not part

of our material, sensible world. He may be present in
terms of His causality and His providential ordering of
the universe, but we are not directly aware of this as
we are of the presence of other persons in our world.
The second and more profound difficulty is that God,
since He is infinite, cannot reveal Himself as He
really is without destroying our autonomy and our freedom.

> Only when we ourselves voluntarily recognize God
> desiring to enter into relationship with Him, can
> our knowledge of Him be compatible with our freedom,
> and so with our existence as personal beings.[30]

Yet this God, hidden by the necessity of His infinite nature, does seem to provide traces of Himself
compatible with our finitude and our freedom. There is
a natural disposition in man for religion. Throughout
his history man has been keenly aware of his dependence
and his inadequacy to such an extent that he has consistently looked beyond himself for help in his help-
lessness. The expressions of this realization have been
many and varied, but by and large the realization is
there. From this viewpoint religion in its widest
sense might well be described as the belief that man's
environment is other and greater than it seems, that
there is above and beyond the natural another order of
being to which men must relate themselves. Atheism can
hardly be called the normal human attitude.

Hick, however, realizes the difficulty in ex-
plaining faith in God as an option voluntarily accepted,
as an attitude which can only be justified subjectively
and for which no demonstrative argument can be cited.
Others have admitted that such an option is a plaus-
ible one, but they also insist that such a view applies
only to this world. In other words, it is a view which
terminates in nature and in no way asserts anything
meaningful about a transcendent Being. In this sense
John Dewey has been willing to speak of God as a purely subjective ideal toward which man tends, but the
only reality such an ideal has is as a never to be
achieved final fulfillment of the natural process. God
is only a way of speaking about the as yet unsolved mys-
teries of nature, or the expression of an aesthetic

attitude which enables one to live more serenely in the
world and more compatibly with his fellow men. Religion is a cultural phenomenon which nourishes and
strengthens man's moral sense. But it begins and ends
there.

One can recall at this point J. Wisdom's well-
known parable of the garden.[31] Just as the garden in
question appears the same to both travelers, so the
world will continue to be the world, whether there is a
God or not. It depends purely and simply on how one
looks at the evidence at hand, what he is willing to
stress or leave unstressed, that determines whether or
not he will settle for a gardener or a God. So, too,
just as nothing will convince the one traveler that
there is no gardener, neither will anything convince
the theist that there is no God.[32] But then we may
very well get to the point where words fail to mean anything anymore and one is left with a totally subjective
attitude which has not the slightest chance of being
verified. But the theist continues to insist that his
religious faith in God is some sort of knowledge of a
real Being, that it is not just a pious interpretation
of the world, not a kind of social good will which enables him to live better with others.

Hick is searching, then, for some kind of verifiability for the proposition, God exists. The theist,
when he speaks of belief in God, means to assert that
there really is a transcendent Being Who manifests Himself through the medium of the finite. But how can
such an assertion look toward any sort of verification?
Hick's answer is to point toward an indirect verification in the lives of theists, and to suggest further
that the theistic position can look to future verification. Admittedly such future verification is only a
possibility at present; but the possibility is there,
and no logic can show that it contains any intrinsic
contradiction.

The theist who takes his position seriously has
a different view of the world than does the atheist,
and this view is translated into his actual life situation. While he may walk the same road as the atheist,
the believer expects that road to lead him eventually

to a heavenly city. He faces the joys and sorrows of
the journey differently. He sees difficulty as a test
of his courage and stamina. Evil he sees as necessarily
giving way to greater good. He can speak of blessings
and purposefulness, of order and happiness, at least at
the end. He has a hope for a future in which all that
is good and noble, all that is true and beautiful, will
be preserved and taken up into a higher level of lasting reality. And someday the journey will end. The
last turn in the road will be taken. At that point his
belief will actually be verified or not. In the mean-
time there is an actual, verifiable difference in the
way the believer thinks and acts which separates him
from the non-believer.

Hick further insists that there is no logical
contradiction involved in either the notion of survival after bodily death or in that of the resurrection
to a new form of life.[33] He does suggest a problem
which might occur in this future life. How is one to
know even there that there is a God and that the sought-
after fulfillment has taken place? Or better, perhaps,
how will one be able to verify personally that he was
right all along, that there really is a kingdom of God
and that he is sharing in it? There is also no logical
contradiction involved in speculating that such a
future state might be just as problematical as this one.
If we do become participators in the kingdom of God,
an infinite God would still be incapable of revealing
Himself for what He is to limited, finite minds. The
difficulty is not all that serious. There is certainly
a difference between knowing that there is a God and
what God is in His divine nature. Our knowing process
operates constantly like this. We have no difficulty
in asserting that there are material objects or that
people are alive. Yet no one is able to define fully
what is meant by matter or life.

But the better answer lies within the realm of
faith itself. There is the incarnate Christ, Jesus of
Nazareth. This Son of the Father came precisely to
teach us of His Father and to show us the way which
leads to Him. Christ Himself has promised that He will
be there and will occupy a special place in His Father's
kingdom.

Within Christianity it is possible to talk about the
infinite God, incomprehensible though He still remains because he has become finitely incarnate in
Jesus of Nazareth. That is to say, God identified
as the Being about Whom Jesus taught and whose attitude to mankind was expressed in Jesus' deeds.
Building upon Jesus' teaching together with that of
the Hebrew prophets before him, Christian theologians
have developed the philosophical conception of this
Being as infinite, uncreated, eternal, and so on.
But the starting point and basis of the Christian
use of the word 'God' remains the historical figure
of Jesus, as known through the New Testament records.
Under his impact we come (in some degree and at some
times) to experience life in a distinctively new way,
as living in the presence of the God whose love was
revealed in the words and actions of Jesus. Is the
appropriateness of this response to the haunting
figure of Jesus--this response of personal disciple-
ship, of acceptance of his teaching, and of coming
to experience life in its relation to 'the God and
Father of our Lord Jesus Christ'--in any way verifiable by future events? Surely our participation in
an eschatological situation in which the reality of
God's loving purpose for us is confirmed by its fulfillment in a heavenly world, and in which the authority of Jesus, and thus of his teaching, is confirmed by his exalted place in that world, would
properly count as confirmatory. It would not (to
repeat) amount to logical demonstration, but it
would constitute a situation in which the grounds
for rational doubt which obtain in the present life
would have been decisively removed. Such eschatological expectations--without the detailed imagery in
which earlier ages have clothed them--are an in-
tegral part of the total Christian conception of
God and his activity. And they suffice, I suggest,
to insure the factual, true-or-false character of
the claim that God, as so conceived, exists.[34]

CONCLUSION

Those who hold the more traditional position on
the nature of the act of faith will find neither Niebuhr's nor Hick's approach very satisfactory. It certainly lacks the objective surety of a valid demon-

stration for the existence of God. When the divine existence itself is included within the act of faith, the theistic position seems to become much more tenuous. So also do further acts of faith in truths revealed by God. Despite the assertion of both Neibuhr and Hick that faith reaches out to a transcendent Being and affirms the transcendent reality of such a Being, they also acknowledge that there is no way to prove this. Hence, there is no real way to keep such an assertion from sinking into fideism and subjectivism, at least in the eyes of a non-believer. But there is no way at all to make the position stronger, based as it is upon the assumption that Kant had made every attempt to demonstrate the existence of God an impossibility.

One gets the impression, too, that Hick, especially, is overly concerned about making the verifiability principle of the analytic philosophers applicable to his logic of faith. He obviously does a more than creditable job in taking the analysts on their own ground and indicating that the proposition, God exists, is verifiable when taken in its context; or, at least that it is not falsifiable. But the theist cannot avoid the uneasy feeling that the position as stated simply removes the whole question of the reality of God out of the reach of the atheist. It puts the existence of a transcendent God on a level from which the non-believer is excluded by definition. It seems to abandon the whole realm of reason, at least in this area, to the atheist and flee to a secret place where only the initiate may enter.

But the position is not without its strong points. Perhaps most important of all it presents a clear explanation of the way the believer's mind works. The person who accepts a God on faith does, as a matter of fact, look at the world, himself and others in a way uniquely different from that of the atheist. There is a certainty about his assertion, a personal relationship to a personal God, a hope for the future which nothing can shake. Any believer will recognize these characteristics of his faith. Nor would anyone deny that the assent to God's existence can be, and often is, based solely on faith; and, further, that such an assent is in very many cases an entirely free option.

That such an assent also produces in the mind of the believer the attitude which has been described is also beyond question.

Another strength of the position is its deep realization of the personal relationship established between the believer and God. What is affirmed is not the Pure Act of the philosophers but the reality of a Being Who is _my_ God. As a result it leads to a dedication and a commitment which can and does transform individual lives. Such a transformation is, in the eyes of the believer, as direct an experience of God as is possible in this life. This approach also avoids long, technical arguments which often produce more harm than good for those not so inclined. Again, it is only fair to acknowledge that even those who insist that the existence of God can be philosophically demonstrated in most cases approached Him first through faith. And for the believer, at least, the most important thing is to get to God and to see the world and himself from that viewpoint. The possibility of a complete and lasting human fulfillment is in the long run the most important factor in the life of any human being.

NOTES

[1] St. Thomas Aquinas, *Summa Theologica*, II-II, 1-7.

[2] *Cf.*, Gabriel Marcel, *Being and Having*, trans. by K. Farrer (London, A & C Black, Ltd. 1949).

[3] C. Cirne-Lima, *Personal Faith*, trans. by G. R. Dimler, S.J. (N.Y., Herder and Herder, 1965).

[4] B. Pascal, *Pensees*, trans. by W. F. Trotter (London, J. M. Dent & Sons, Ltd., 1931) pp. 52 ff.

[5] William James, *The Will to Believe* (Dover Publications, 1956); *cf.*, also, my *God and the Empiricists* (Milwaukee, Wis., Bruce Publishing Company, 1968), Ch. IV.

[6] *Ibid.*, p. 22.

[7] *Ibid.*, p. 25.

[8] *Ibid.*, p. 26.

[9] *Ibid.*, p. 27.

[10] *Ibid.*, p. 29.

[11] John Hick, *Faith and Knowledge* (Ithaca, N.Y., Cornell University Press, 1966), p. 44.

[12] H. Richard Niebuhr, *The Meaning of Revelation* (N.Y., The Macmilland Company, 1941).

[13] *Ibid.*, p. 15.

[14] *Ibid.*, p. 16.

[15] *Ibid.*, p. 19.

[16] *Ibid.*, pp. 30-31.

[17] *Ibid.*, p. 91.

[18]Ibid., p. 104.

[19]Ibid., p. 111.

[20]Ibid., p. 121.

[21]Ibid., p. 126.

[22]Ibid., p. 133.

[23]Ibid., p. 138.

[24]Summa Contra Gentiles, I, 4.

[25]John Hick, Faith and Knowledge (Ithaca, N.Y., Cornell University Press, 1966).

[26]Ibid., p. 99.

[27]Ibid., p. 104.

[28]Ibid., p. 113.

[29]Ibid., pp. 114-115.

[30]Ibid., p. 134.

[31]Cf., Logic and Language, ed. A. G. N. Flew (Oxford, 1951).

[32]Cf., A. G. N. Flew's essay, "Theology and Falsification," in New Essays in Philosophical Theology, ed. A. G. N. Flew and A. C. MacIntyre (London, 1955).

[33]J. Hick, op. cit., Ch. 8.

[34]Ibid., pp. 198-199.

VI

THE GOD WITHIN

THE DIVINE PRESENCE

In the approaches to God which have been considered in the previous chapters there are common characteristics which appear consistently. With the possible exception of Bernhardt there is no attempt to establish the divine existence on the basis of demonstrative proof. While Newman does not reject the possibility of such a proof, he sees it only as one way--and not exactly the usual way, at that--by which human beings arrive at the conviction that God exists. The sense of the divine presence judging one's actions with approval or disapproval is always more instrumental in turning the individual toward the God Who constantly works through human conscience. The same divine presence, while less personal, is, nevertheless, a heritage of the race according to Jung; just as it is there directing man to his evolutionary perfection in Teilhard de Chardin. At appears, too, in both Kierkegaard and Niebuhr, since the theistic view of the world is always based on more than a pure option, a simple choosing of one alternative over another. Such an option may be a "leap" in the Kierkegaardian sense, but one must still be drawn to make such a leap. The same is true of Hick in his discussion of faith on the espistemological level. There is always a value involved in adopting such a view of the world, and to accept this view of the world as a value necessarily connects it with the source of good and the ground of all value.

In all cases but one this presence is a personal one. It leads to an affirmation of "my God" rather than to a God. It is I, not just man, who am the accountable one; it is my faith that gives me a whole different outlook on the world. And this faith in turn is grounded in a personal "Thou" Who is present to me and yet transcends me. One no longer sins against the law but against Another Who legislates for my good in order to bring me to Himself.

GOD AS IMMANENT

It is true further, that if God is present, turning individuals to Himself, then in a sense He is immanent to the world. Yet His immanence always remains a hidden one; for, otherwise, the free option which the individual is required to make would become impossible. The affirmation of immanence is quite clear in Newman, in Kierkegaard, and in Niebuhr, as it is in Jung. In Teilhard de Chardin it is manifested in man's drive toward spirit, toward the Omega Point which already exists as Alpha, the Beginning.

Again, however, an exception must be made in the case of Bernhardt. While he argues for the immanent presence of God in the world, he does so in a highly impersonal fashion, and it is not at all clear that God is a personal being. The Directional Momentum he speaks of may be at the heart of the universe, but it can hardly be said to appeal to men's hearts. The reality of such a source is affirmed as an argumentative conclusion and is not readily apparent to anyone who does not seek it philosophically. Nor does such a reality seem to transcend the universe in any way. And it could hardly do so, since it is by definition the immanent source of all that is. And the universe is all that there is.

GOD AS TRANSCENDENT

For all the others God is transcendent as well as immanent. This transcendence is manifested in two ways. In the first place God transcends man. He either judges man or is that toward which man strives in hope of the perfection which will one day be his. For Jung God broods over the race, and the race carries the image of God with it, however cryptically that image may appear. Yet it is there turning man from his finitude and his incompleteness to the hidden source of his reality and the promise of something better. For Teilhard de Chardin God is spirit moving across time, beckoning man to reflective awareness and thus to ever greater perfection, and to ultimate fulfillment.

But there is more than this. For God not only stands outside of man but also outside of time and space, beyond even the universe of His creation. He remains

the absolute Other, the beginning and the end, the all-
perfect in contrast to the partiality and the finitude
which man finds all around him as well as in himself.
In Niebuhr God is the You which completes every I, the
personal Absolute Who must become my God at the price
of remaining forever alien. For Newman He is the ultimate rewarder of every good conscience. For Kierkegaard He is the personal goal that justifies and makes
reasonable every commitment to seeming absurdity.

And this is necessary, even if we grasp only
darkly what we mean, when we affirm such an absolute.
There is a tendency today in some theistic circles to
see God only as a human value; to regard Him, for example, only as man's fulfillment in a finite situation.
Hence, the temptation arises to speak of Him only in
univocal human terms and to brush all else aside as
meaningless. The suggestion is there that it is enough
to see God in our brother, as the peace that comes to
the human heart that acknowledges Him, as the security
and hope that those who serve Him possess. God may
well transcend the finite, but the finite can do no
more than react to the finite manifestations of His
reality. To attempt to speak of such a God in any
other way would be to lose track of what we are saying.

But one can admit that our understanding of God
is limited and finite (what else could it be?) without
affirming that we can suspect nothing more. One can
also agree that whatever contact we presently make with
God is always on a human level without seeming to reduce God to the human status. We recognize the mysterious in other areas of life and the inadequacy of
either our intellects or our language to deal with it.
Why should we demand here a clarity of thought and
language, when we are quite willing to admit the impossibility of such in philosophy and art, in literature, and even in science? Once we are willing to admit
the evidence of the reality of a transcendent Being,
then it becomes more reasonable to make whatever use we
can of inadequate language, of incomplete concepts, than
to ignore the transcendence of such a Being, or to anthropomorphize Him to such lengths as to literally de-
prive Him of His own unique mode of existence. To use
language imaginatively or analogously or even negatively

may not provide us with a science of God, but it will keep us aware that we know _that_ He is even if we do not know _what_ He is. A theism that is willing to speak of God only univocally and to attribute to Him only so much reality as can be expressed by our language may very well find itself accused of idolatry, and the **very** worst kind of that--self-idolatry.

GOD AS SOURCE OF ORDER

There is quite common agreement among the theists whose writings have been considered that the recognition of God involves the further realization that the universe is an ordered universe with everything in it working toward a destined end. Hence, the universe is purposeful and meaningful. It follows that there is a reason for man's place in it; that what he does counts; that his options are more than mere velleities; and that he has a place in the scheme of things. However hidden this purposefulness may seem at times, the theist has the assurance that nothing happens in vain, that good will somehow triumph over evil, and that the reasoned, virtuous life is not just its own reward.

It is a universe, too, in which hope predominates; for there is the grounded trust that success will one day crown the work. Beauty, truth and goodness are values that will be preserved. The good life in the highest sense is worth striving for, because whatever is achieved will endure. There is an antidote here for all the ills that flesh is heir to, for the situation is in control and with Socrates one can affirm that nothing evil can happen to a good man either in life or in death.

The theistic option, too, reaffirms man's freedom and makes him in a radical sense the master of his own destiny. It gives him the chance to develop a mature sense of responsibility and urges him toward a selfless rather than a selfish love. Especially in Kierkegaard and in Niebuhr the free opening of oneself to the eternal Person leads the individual to an opening of himself to others. The contact between himself and the eternal Thou makes one aware of the worth and dignity of all otherness. There has to arise out of such recognition a different attitude toward society and its meaning. To see how radically different such

an attitude is one need only compare it to the Sartrean
position of ultimate absurdity and the threat of "the
other."

FAITH AND REASON

In most of the authors very little separation is
made between faith and reason. Hick, for example, puts
faith into the context of a natural epistemology. Whatever theological difficulties may technically arise
here, it is true that both faith and reason contribute
to the theist's view of his life in the world. There
is a similarity to Augustine's dictum, Fides quaerens
intellectum, in so far as faith is at times presupposed
while reason seeks to understand what it believes. At
the same time there is reason striving to indicate that
it is good and worthwhile and even more reasonable to
believe.

The appeal of such an approach to God is grounded
in its unwillingness to fragment man, and its awareness
that a more narrow approach is always a dehumanization.
Intellect alone may very well be able to demonstrate
God's existence, but proof may not reach far enough to
produce the good man; and theists are expected to practice goodness as well as affirm its value. A blind
choice of God in no way founded on reason is hardly
tenable, while an emotional approach is certainly not
fully human. But to recognize that all three factors
are components of the human make-up and to appeal to
all of them in confronting man with the God-question is
not only eminently reasonable but thoroughly human. And
the question of the existence or the nonexistence of God
is uniquely and fundamentally a human one. God certainly knows that He exists.

Newman neither specifically includes nor excludes faith, when he deals with the God of conscience.
But his whole approach, as we have seen is grounded not
on conclusive demonstration but on the inescapable evidence of God's presence to the human conscience. Kierkegaard makes faith an essential element of man's acceptance of God, and he comes closest, perhaps, to making
faith an irrational act. But this is true only from the
viewpoint of the unbeliever who feels such a commitment
humanly unreasonable. The seeming absurdity of such an

act is resolved when it is made in and through faith.
Niebuhr, too, will accept no other approach to the true
God and insists that faith is essential and must occur
within a revelatory context. Hick would presumably
take the same position since he does not think there is
a conclusive demonstration for the existence of God.
He is careful, however, to insist that the act of faith
is certainly based on and includes a reasoning process.

MAN'S RESPONSE
        As we have seen, an integral part of such a
theistic position is the response it is meant to evoke
from man. Man is no longer just a philosopher demon-
strating the existence of a Being distinct from the
world, dwelling in the lonely splendor of Pure Act.
God is a Person Who initiates contact with man and Who
asks the free commitment of the individual self. It is
a call to recognition, to submission, an invitation to
look upon the universe in all the ways that have been
described and to accept one's destiny as unalterably
linked with God. It demands an ever increasing openness to the primal source of all things and a corresponding openness to others. There is a shattering of
isolation and alienation, so that man becomes in
Aquinas's phrase, "capax Dei."

        The importance of such a response can hardly be
over-emphasized. It is not by intellectual recognition
alone that man achieves the happiness promised him, but
by a total giving of himself to the divine plan and its
ultimate purpose in decreeing the reality of the finite.
A creating God must order all things to Himself because
He alone is ultimate meaning and reality. It is only
fitting that beings should return to Being, and that
free personal beings should return there freely and in
personal commitment. Niebuhr is correct when he asserts
that God has to become "my God," if theism is to be a
living force in one's life.

THE FLIGHT FROM PROOF
        There is no proof for the existence of God in
either the Old or the New Testament. The arguments are
formulated later, particularly with St. Augustine and
still later with the great Scholastic theologians of
the Middle Ages. William of Ockham was probably the

first of the Scholastics to deny that the proofs were valid. Hume certainly cast doubt on the possibility of proving that there is a God. But it was the German philosopher, Kant, who has had the greatest influence on subsequent philosophy and its suspicion of the validity of any proof for God's existence. Whatever one may think of the Kantian objections to the proofs, as he knew them, it is a fact that since Kant there has been a decided lack of interest in an approach to God based on demonstration. Kant's rejection resulted first of all in a retreat to faith, to sentimentalism, and to areas where the theist could not really be touched by attacks based on philosophic reason. Pascal's dictum, the heart has reasons which the reason knows not, is apropos here. The corresponding flowering of both scientific and philosophical materialism in the nineteenth century coupled with the rise of religious modernism left the field of reason practically deserted by the traditional theists. If there is a renewal of theism today, or at least a renewal of the search for the transcendent and the non-experienceable, it is not based on new insights into the validity of philosophical demonstration.

It seems to be based, rather, on a new insight into man and the need he has to salvage his own humanity. There are reasons for this. One of the foremost is the new technocracy which has permeated our society. Enough has been written about its de-humanizing effect on the individual without having to recall it here. Suffice it to say that contemporary man is frightened by it, feels he has no part in it, and is fairly sure that it will not only continue but begin to pervade more and more areas of his life, and eventually go on without him. However many have been the benefits of such a society, and they have been many, the ordinary man thinks that the experts, the leaders of the technology, will continue to act more as experts than as men. When scientific progress and economic viability become the norms for functioning, and human values are placed second in importance to these, the question about the significance of human individuality and the value of the person is bound to arise.

THE DECLINE OF THE PERSONAL

When the question does arise for the individual, he confronts a disturbing fact. As more and more power becomes available to the technocratic society, the individual becomes increasingly powerless to have any say about its use. He has almost everything done for him. He is told what to eat, what to wear, what sort of a house to live in, what kind of a car to drive, what toothpaste to use, etc. As a member of that society he is committed to space, to foreign wars, to welfare programs without ever being consulted. His taxes help pay for trips to the moon, but the closest he gets to being involved is the view on television. He can cast his vote for the candidate of his choice, but he is informed ahead of time what candidate will win. Even his moral codes and religious attitudes are prescribed for him in magazines and commercials. In other words, the individual pays for the power and the convenience with the surrender of most of his ability to control the process.

Now much of this is unavoidable in a society as complex as ours, but it is also understandable why there should be a growing resentment and even rebellion against a system which seems to leave so little room for the individual's personal goals and human development. Even those who rebel do not often know before which building in the complex they should be carrying their signs. In the past one was referred to the philospher or the theologian for a deeper understanding of man and his human condition. But today many philosophers have retreated to the comparative safety of linguistic analysis and more than a few theologians are chanting the liturgy of a secularized Christianity before the grave of a dead God.

It has been suggested that the twentieth century is uniquely different from past ages. In other cultures--that of the ancient world, for example, the Middle Ages and the Renaissance--there were always presumptions on which the cultures were based and which were consciously or unconsciously accepted by the individuals. In a time of crisis the individual could turn to these assumptions, reorientate himself with reference to them, and make use of them to live with, if not solve, his personal anxiety. In our age it is precisely the assumptions of our culture which are being questioned and denied so that the individual of the twentieth century literally has no way to turn in his personal anxiety and no norms that he can use as a solution to his personal disturbance.

It is no wonder, then, that some people should begin to have a real fear of what will happen to them as individuals. The ultimate danger that threatens is that people will eventually cease to think and will surrender themselves to convenience, to the well-provided life, without question and without the responsibility which is the necessary counterpart of human freedom. What a man has, the possessions he acquires, and the prestige he achieves through things become more important than what he really is on the human level. Having is substituted for being. Now if there is anything which differentiates man from all the other species, it is his capacity for reflective awareness and his ability to commit himself responsibly and freely to what he sees must reasonably be done. Among the animals, man alone has a sense of history and an awareness of time. He alone feels guilt, quails before the knowledge of his own mortality, can smile at the incongruous and the unexpected. He alone knows the difference between what he can do and what he ought to do. All these are values that must be maintained. William F. Lynch puts it quite clearly in his book, Christ and Prometheus.

I am concerned with the fundamental endlessness of a secularity cut off from the broad totality of human sensibility. This counterimage comes out more clearly when we turn to the world of objects. Something that preoccupies many a modern artist is any endless proliferation of objects that has its own separate life and unconditionality, an independent world with no relation to the human. Sheer proliferation is a frequent image. In Ionesco, it is chairs, chairs, chairs, chairs, chairs, in a riotous image of the point. In Sartre it is this endless proliferation of things, like a jungle that in its growth will finally conquer the city of man, that is part of the cause of the nausea at things.

*   *   *   *

Here the image I want myself to recall is my own
image of the cosmological. To the degree that this
unconditional nonhuman proliferation of objects develops, you get the return of another form of the
cosmological situation for man. But instead of being a pinpoint lost in awful space among the endless
stars, he feels himself thus situated in a new world
of objects and sensations. He has not yet forced
the new world into his terms. He has not yet built
an inside that can handle the great new world.
there are too many things, too many people, too many
sensations, too many alternatives for action. It
seems impossible to stop the proliferation, the es-
calation, the endlessness. The stars were a minor
cosmological problem and never bothered men as much
as we say they did, and there was this obvious advantage about the stars that they provided space to
breathe. But now there is no space left; it has
been taken away by objects; nobody knows how to turn
the process off; there is the beginning of an alto-
gether new kind of cosmological insecurity in the
air; there is a subterranean panic that does not yet
call itself by that name because it hides itself under the form of violence, as insecurity always does.

(Christ and Prometheus, University of Notre
Dame Press, Notre Dame, Ind., 1970, p. 88.)

SALVAGING THE HUMAN
     It becomes at least understandable, then, why
contemporary writers and artists tend to put the stress
on the salvation of man rather than on a transcendent
God. One must preserve the human before one can turn
to what transcends the human. A metaphysical proof
that all is well makes little impact. All is not well.
And human reason balks at the inhumanity it finds on
the human level. There can be little relish for metaphysics and perhaps even little concern about the possibility of a transcendent Being, when the disturbance
and the perplexity are so radically connected with the
fundamental emotional need for security and individual
integrity.

The danger here is apparent enough. It is to
seek some sort of human salvation entirely on the human level. The tendency to substitute the human for
the divine is never far from us. In more recent times
Dewey gave it a modern expression. He did it by capi-
talizing on the human awareness of the value and dignity involved in being human. Dewey failed primarily
because his attempt was overweighted on the side of
science as a means to bring about and preserve the human values we all prize so highly. Contemporary humanists are much more skeptical about the salvific
virtue of the scientific method.

L. Bagolini in an article published in 1968 en-
titled "Ateismo e Scienze Sociali" points out that a
humanism based on a scientific approach will lead in-
evitably to what it reacts against. (Quaderni de
Cultura, 11, serie 5, Scuola Cattolica di Cultura;
Udine, Italy, 1968.) One can say what one wishes about
the impersonalism of the machine and the inhumanity of
the technocratic society. One can make a plea for man
against those who would dehumanize him. But to look
for the preservation of all that is best in man only on
the human level is to assert that man and his human
condition are capable of being totally explained in
terms of human reason. In Gabriel Marcel's words, it
makes man a problem to be solved rather than a mystery
to be explored. It is theoretically possible to solve
any problem. If the solution is best achieved by the
application of the scientific method, then the reasonable approach is for man to submit himself to that
method rather than to fight against it. The results,
however, of such a submission may well be disastrous.
For the machine, the computer, is precisely the expression of this attitude that everything can be ration-
alized. This had to lead eventually to a completely
"reasonable" society in which there is no longer any
place for decision or free choice. All the alternatives
will have been "reasonably" plotted and reduced to one,
obviously the "most reasonable." It will make no sense
one day to speak of individual responsibility or of
weighty decisions. All human appetites, all the in-
tangibles that give rise to art, to literature, to
philosophy--the values most prized by the humanists--
will be scientifically predicted and technically satis-

fied. No humanism grounded in a scientific methodology
can stand up to that.

There is another way to go. One can insist that
however tied to earth man is by reason of his origin
and his destiny, there is something about the human
which will defy the attempts of science to reduce it to
a problem capable of scientific investigation and solution. Man's aesthetic sense, his capacity for reflective thought, his awareness of himself as freedom, his
recognition of his own mortality, all mark him off as a
unique species on the earth. Given time he will learn
to moderate his kinship with the beasts and turn to the
development of those human qualities that seem capable
of endless development.

Such a humanism is not particularly theistic. It
is probably more agnostic than atheistic; but its emphasis is on man, and its dream is to make man fully
human. I dislike using the term, secularistic humanism,
but, perhaps, it comes closest to summarizing the position, at least in attempting to differentiate it from a
humanism which is fully and explicitly theistic. The
differentiation, however, has to be qualified. Both
types of humanism have many things in common. Both desire, for example, to see the full flowering of those
characteristics which must be preserved at all costs.
Where they differ, they differ radically, of course;
but they can find a common ground in their struggle to
resist whatever is a threat to man. As William Lynch
again points out:

> True secularity has more often been an attack on in-
> human forms of the cosmological than it has been an
> attack on religion. I repeat that we ought to ex-
> periment with a reading of much of the history of the
> secular project as a series of attacks on intoler-
> able, nonhuman forms of the cosmological. If secular-
> ity were to find in religion a form of the cosmologi-
> cal that is not a threat to man, a form that would
> instead be foundation and guarantee of the project,
> then history might reach another significant mile-
> stone--a milestone of collaboration with old reli-
> gious enemies and an end to some of the painful divi-
> sions of the intelligence in our culture.
> (Lynch, William, op. cit., p. 124.)

I think the statement is true, and that both secularistic and theistic humanists would be better off to join forces in fighting a common threat. Human values possess intrinsic worth, and, looked at simply from a human viewpoint, it makes more sense to fight to maintain them than to divide on their ultimate source and so be conquered. At the same time I think that the position one takes on the ultimate ground of such values has to be considered, if for no other reason than to make contemporary humanism as viable and as realistic as possible. It is from this point of view that I think secular humanism is open to question. For while it is based on the unique value of the human, it has to insist that such values will not only survive but are capable of being indefinitely developed. And here one may well pause. The difficulty has been that so far in the history of the human species, with rare exceptions, the capacity has remained just that—a capacity. The progress we can point to over the centuries has by and large occurred most strikingly and most dramatically in those areas that are not regarded as totally human—at least in the humanistic sense. Practical and theoretical science, material convenience, military power, economic improvement, all these have had a history of almost miraculous success. Yet these are precisely the areas which are seen as a threat to man in his humanity. In age after age the artist, the philosopher, the poet, the theologian have cried out and they continue to cry out against the suffering, the savagery, the inhumanity of man to man. In this area the race does not seem to have come very far. We are still struggling to be human even while we ready space ships to the moon. There seems to be an incorrigibility about this species that makes it impossible for us to learn very much from the past and makes it necessary for us to start our trek toward salvation from an individual and a human point of view not very different from that of our ancestors.

There is, for example, very little difference between us and our forefathers in our yearning for the good life and our recognition of the prestige and the convenience that wealth can bring. We have not been exempted in any marked degree from either their selfishness or their greed. Plutarch's description of Alcibiades standing on the lead ship as the Athenian fleet left to conquer Sicily is not inappropriate today.

He had a golden shield made for himself, bearing no ancestral device, but an Eros armed with a thunderbolt. (<u>Plutarch's Lives</u>, the Loeb Classical Edition, vol. 4, Harvard University Press, Cambridge, Mass., 1959, p. 41.)

We may have learned how to make war more effectively, and we are able to employ more sophisticated weapons (and more inhuman ones), but the greed and the lust for power are pretty much the same. One could cite countless examples. And there are examples on the side of humaneness also. Enough, it is true, to enable us to hope that more are still possible. But in general the evidence is there that man has not changed very much in his history on this planet.

In other words our search for human values and the ability to maintain them has to be worked out more on the individual than on the specific human level. The great humanists have recognized this and are as much aware of human fallibility and inadequacy as they are of man's grandeur and his capacity for the heroic. The grandeur and the heroism are there, but they are not nearly as evident nor as consistently a part of most men's lives as are the fallibility and the inadequacy. It seems, too, that most men are more interested in finding a remedy for their failure than they are in achieving brilliant success.

THEISTIC HUMANISM
It is in this particular area that I suggest a theistic humanism is both more realistic and more viable. It takes man as it finds him and points him beyond himself to a transcendent goal which is the ultimate remedy for all the partiality and imperfection with which we are so familiar. It is too realistic to raise hopes for an earthly utopia, because it knows what is in man. It also recognizes the human yearning for what is better, and it promises fulfillment based on a striving that will always be partial and imperfect. Such a humanism places more faith in God than it does in man. Yet it does not advocate a flight from the human situation, nor does it see human society as hopeless. There is after all one way to human fulfillment, and that is in and through the human situation. But it

does not pretend that the situation is other than it is. It opens man to otherness, to the Divine, to a healing view of himself and his world which each man desperately needs.

I am suggesting that theistic humanism is better simply because it is more human. It affirms all the human values without encountering the danger of losing them, because it grounds them in an eternal source. Without detracting from the human or the finite, it looks beyond both the human and the finite for an explanation of their ultimate value. This is the view of man and his world which is characteristic of the people whose writings we have considered in this book. The last statement may need some qualification with regard to Bernhardt, but at least he does not leave man entirely to his own devices. Further, there is in the theistic approaches studied a willingness to see man as capable of progress and achievement, if he will only maintain an openness to the God Who is present to him from within. Whether such openness be conceived as an awareness of accountability, as a call to faith and hope, as a dim consciousness of one's origins, or as an insight into a future perfectibility, all of this can only make a man walk more humanly in a situation where the great temptation is to explain that situation only in its own terms. Perhaps the best thing that can be said about theistic humanism is that it refuses to condemn man to himself.

verification of God's existence, 120
Hugh of St. Victor, 49, 50
Human Consciousness, 73-96, 131
Humanism, 88, 92; secularistic, 138,139; theistic, 138-141
Hume, David, 18, 133; on the Argument from Design, 5, 6; constant association of ideas, 3; philosophical skepticism, 3
Hyper-personal, 94

Idea of a University, 23
Iliff Review, 60
Illative sense, 19
Immortality, of souls, 100; see Transeunce
Impositionalism, 65
Individual, in Kierkegaard, 29, 30, 33, 37, 39, 41, 50-51, 53
The Individual and His Religion, 76
Inference, 19
Ionesco, 135
Irrationalism, 48, 50
Isaac, 52

James, William, 60, 75, 103-106; materialism, 105; theistic option, 105
Jaspers, 29
Job, and the experience of God, 80, 81
Journals, 49, 50
Jung, Carl G., 73, 75, 78-85, 96, 127, 128; collective unconsciousness, 78-79, 80, 82; death of God, 79; dreams, 79-80, 81; ego, 83; individual consciousness, 78; person 83;

quaternity, 79, 83; self, 83; symbols, 79, 82

Kant, Immanuel, 82, 106-107, 112, 123, 133; on the Argument from Design, 5-6
Kierkegaard, Søren, 29-56, 127, 128, 129, 130, 131; the Absurd, 48, 49, 50; on Consciousness, 34; criticism of objective truth, 35; despair, 34, 37; essential knowledge, 35-36; leap into sin, 40; leap of faith, 37, 49; love, 47; on man 33, 40; objections to secularized Christianity, 31; personal subjectivity, 35, 38, 54; reason, 45-47, 49, 52; rejection of Hegelianism, 30; on self, 33; on spirit, 33, and soul-body relation, 40-41

Locke, 3, 17
Logic, 7, 14-16; assumptions of, 15; syllogistic reasoning, 14
Love, and Kierkegaard, 47
Luther, Martin, 31, 32, 106
Lynch, William F., 135, 138

Marcel, Gabriel, 29, 101, 137
Marxism, 92
Mathematics, 18
The Meaning of Revelation, 107
Metaphysics, 64, 70, 71, 101, 136
Middle Ages, 134

Mill, 5
Modality, category of, 68, 69; concept of, 65
Modifiability, 66, 69
Moral law, 111-113, 118
Mount Moriah, 52
Multiplicity, 67, 69
Mynster, Bishop, 31

Newman, John Henry, 1-23, 90, 128, 129, 131; awareness of own existence, 8-9; complex propositions, 13; definition of consciousness, 9, 16; individual consciousness, 21, 23; nature of assent, 7-8, 11, 17, 19, 21; notion of finite being, 2; notional assent, 2, 6; notional propositions, 7, 8, 20; order, 5, 6; personal obligation imposed by Personal Being, 13; real propositions, 7; religion, 12; simple propositions, 13; taste, 9, 22, 23
Newton, 18
Niebuhr, H. Richard, 107-115, 122, 123, 127, 128, 129, 130, 132; God as person, 114; historical relativism, 107; knowledge of things, 109; knowledge of persons, 110; on the philosophical demonstration of God, 100; revelation, 108-109, 110
Noosphere, 94, 95

Ockham, 132-133
Omega point, 89, 90, 94, 95, 128
Ontological argument, 45,46

Operationalism, according to Bernhardt, 65, 67, 69
Otherness, 67

Paley, William, 1
Paradox, according to Kierkegaard, 49-50, 52
Pascal, Blaise, 102-103, 133; Pascal's wager, 102, 105
The Philosophical Fragments, 43
Physics, 18
Physicotheological argument, see Argument from Design
Plato, Form of the Good, 113
Platonic doctrine of recollection, 43
Plutarch, 139
Plutarch's Lives, 139-140
Predictive possibility, presupposition of, 62; see Bernhardt
Principia, 18
Principle of non-contradiction, 2
Principle of sufficient reason, 2
The Proof of Theism, 9, 13
Propositions, complex, 13; notional, 7, 20; real, 7; simple, 13
Protestantism, 111, 115
Psychiatry, 74
Psychotherapy, 76

Quality, 66, 69
Quaternity, 79, 83

Rahner, Karl, 68
Rationalism, 53